Send for Me:
The McCleary Story

Suzanne R. McCleary

ISBN: 1477618252
ISBN-13: 9781477618257

DEDICATION

For my children, Liam and Bella Ross & my father,
Jack Alexander McCleary

ACKNOWLEDGMENTS

First, thank you to my dear family: David, Bella and Liam Ross for their support and patience during this year of obsessive writing, researching and talking about long lost relatives. You may now have my full attention.

Second, thank you to all of my early readers and encouragers: Christine Coffey, Sundee Shirrod, and David Ross; also to authors Michael Staudinger and Robert X. Cringely for their invaluable guidance.

Third, thanks to my extended family that tolerated my prying interviews and amateur film skills: the late James "Scotty" McCleary, Betty McCleary Roether, and my dad, Jack A. McCleary. Also, to the very much alive, Dona McCleary Belt, Howard D. McCleary, Beverley McCleary Raffety and my mother, Linda Rawlings McCleary.

Thank you to my cousins: Gregg Belt, Scott Richey, Connie Richey, Jeff Reis, and especially Tod Williams for their memories of our grandparents.

Thank you to those who provided their knowledge and insight about the Old Country: Ireland and Scotland, they are Edith Henderson (cousin met through ancestry.com), Malachy McAlonan and Tom O'Riordan.

Special thanks to Jim Watts, his knowledge about the McClearys and the Watts in Butte, Montana and Washington State enriched the story so much.

Thank you to my brother Mike McCleary for reading the finished product for donnybrook fodder. Christy Thompson provided the excellent editing that the story needed to rein it in, I thank her as well.

Finally, deepest gratitude to all my McCleary and Hunter relatives, past and present, for living such remarkable and interesting lives that made writing this story both a pleasure and an honor.

S. McCleary, August 2012

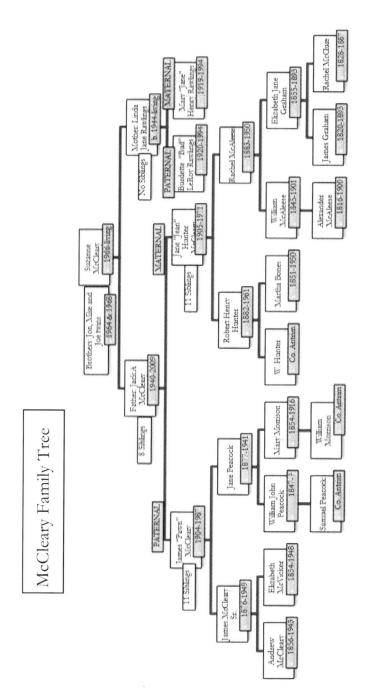

McCleary Family Tree

CHAPTER 1

THE MINE

Going down into the heat of the mine was the worst of it. As the rickety metal cage dropped it got hotter and hotter, almost unbearable; you had to keep your mind under control or the stifling heat alone would make you panic and go nuts. The guys said you were getting closer and closer to hell the further down the cage went in the dark and the hotter it got. 1000 ft...2000 ft....3000 ft... 4000 ft... 1 mile. The medieval-looking steel cage stopped with a hearty jerk at a mile down. They quickly peeled out of the cage like the sections of an orange; one of the men reeking of stale, processed-through-the-pores alcohol from the night before at the pub. The breath of the hung-over was horrid and the cage was small. Occasionally, the coal miners on shift wore raincoats in the cage and as it dropped and got hot, water was poured from above to cool them off and give a tiny bit of relief.

The darkness was disturbing but after working in the coal mines for years you got used to it and it was just part of the job; if you didn't go to work in the dark you didn't feed your family. The only light they had was the one on their miner's helmet, looking like a tarred and greasy Cyclops, and a lantern that every couple of guys carried. Every day when the cage took them back up, eighteen men and boys at a time packed in tight, gripping a bar above their heads, the light at the surface was absolutely blinding, like an explosion. After twelve or fifteen hours underground, the smell of fresh air was foreign and wonderful and the green hills around Harthill, Scotland seemed to sparkle like in the Gaelic folk tales that they told their kids at night.

Some coal miners didn't make it out of the miles of mines that ran beneath most of Lanarkshire, Scotland and James Sr. was used to that. The wives were used to it too; a man or boy was killed in one of many mines in the area nearly every day. Some coal miners were killed at the mouth of the mine, or on the tracks for the coal cars, some fell down the shaft, some were buried deep in the mine when a wall gave way. Many simply went to sleep and dropped where they stood from the poison fumes that they couldn't see but were just as deadly as being hit by a rail car full of coal.

The hardest part of killing rats in the coal mine was cornering the bastards. Once they were in a corner it was easy to dispatch them with the eighteen inches of rubber tubing that the rat killer held in his hand. Such a common thing to use for a weapon, but it worked well and produced less gore than other methods. It took one direct hit with the hose and the big, brown rats with the little faces went down quick. James kicked their limp bodies into the gunny sack with his worn steel toed boot. He didn't like to touch them. The shift boss got killed on the track at the mouth of the mine last week trying to run off some rats, and since then James had been killing the dirty things with a vengeance. As if that would bring the boss back. But the more rats he brought out in the gunny sack at the end of the day, the more likely the walking boss was to notice and move him up to mucker, the next job up on the ladder for a miner.

Ratter was the most disrespected job in the mine. Even the nipper boys with their dirty bare feet sitting in the mine all day opening and closing doors as the coal cars approached, one every couple of hours, got more respect than a rat killer.[1] Rats lived in the mines and travelled in packs looking for crumbs left behind by the miners or oats spilled from the pit ponies food. The only workers held in lower regard than a ratter were the women that worked at the mouth of the mine with dirty skirts hitched up, knees showing and big, high boots on scrawny white legs. The women miners wore filthy shawls wrapped tightly around their heads and shoulders, while they struggled all day to keep the rail cars running and dumping and back onto the right track. Their skirts where tied up to keep them out of the wheels and it wasn't unusual to lose a finger or even a hand at that station.[2] The women working at the mouth of the mine were the lowest of the low, one step away from the prostitutes in Blackridge or Harthill.

In the villages, the female caste system went like this: mothers and housewives, boarding house operators, domestic servants in the city (Edinburgh or Glasgow), workers in the linen and lace mills, barmaids in the taverns, women working the mouth of the mine, and the prostitutes that worked the taverns in town were the most reviled. There was long held belief among miners that if a woman entered the mine it was bad luck and some misfortune would befall one of the men in the mine soon after. Women were banned from the mine proper and only worked at the face, yet tragedy still struck in the Scottish coal mines almost daily.

James McCleary Sr., my great grandfather, was a rat killer. When my grandpa, also called James McCleary, said his dad was a rat killer, I thought it was an Old Country insult or just the trademark McCleary sarcasm. A snarky way of saying the man was an asshole. But James McCleary Sr. of Harthill, Scotland indeed hunted and killed rats in the coal mines around Shotts for a living. Among all the hard jobs in the coal mine in the early 1900s, the job of rat killer was not only difficult, dirty and disgusting but an embarrassment. It wasn't looked upon by the other miners as a real working man's job. Nevertheless, James had a family to support and while living in the miners housing on Victoria Street (not fancy like it sounds) was a roof over their heads, it was not much more.

The McClearys had two rooms for a family of fourteen, no toilet facilities for the women and children; the two, rank outhouses in the street were only for the men. The long suffering wives and mothers that ran these homes had no running water indoors; it was available at two spouts out on the street for 150 people. Rats were underfoot in the houses, rotten garbage and open sewage threatened health in the rows of homes built by the company to house the workers.[3] Many came from far afield in Ireland, England and other parts of Scotland to take advantage of the plentiful work in the coal mines.

My great-grandfather was also a felon. To improve his family's bleak situation James McCleary Sr. tried a short career in the counterfeiting arts. In 1922-23, some of the pits were closing down and people were desperate to feed their families. The McCleary family of fourteen was no different. My clever and enterprising great-grandfather studied and invented a die machine to stamp out the plastic coinage that was used for currency in Scotland in those days. He gathered combs, for the hair, made of Bakelite - a plastic-type substance, and melted those down to press in his machine. He was a smart, creative man and thought he'd devised a way to improve his family's plight for the long term with this excellent machine.

Then he got caught. The plan went sour when James and wife Jane started spending the money like aristocrats. And they definitely were not, anyone that lived in the miners' rows was poor. Mrs. McCleary started wearing new, expensive dresses and an abundance of new, pricey goods started to show up in their house. The authorities in Bathgate, the next town over, became aware of the situation. The McClearys were spending the sham coins in Bathgate rather than Harthill to throw the authorities off their trail. James was arrested and charged with counterfeiting, a felony in Scotland. He was promptly jailed and served out his time for the crime.

On the home front, James McCleary Sr. was a hard man, a cold disciplinarian and "had the emotions of a pig" my grandpa used to say. And great grandpa was a drinker; that's family parlance for a bad alcoholic. The twelve McCleary children of Harthill, Scotland had a difficult life not only living in a poor mining village but under the iron rule of their father - the father with a very bad reputation in the community. But let me back up and begin at the beginning in Ireland.

CHAPTER 2

COUNTY ANTRIM, NORTHERN IRELAND - 1850

The McClearys, my grandpa's family, and the Hunters, my grandma's family, all came from the same place: Slemish Mountain, County Antrim, Northern Ireland and its close environs. Both sides of my dad's family came from this green, lush land of undulating hills and tangled blackberry bush fences called Ulster, in the north of Ireland. In the generations prior to 1850, the McClearys and Hunters were two families farming, mining, making lace and linen, gardening and selling flowers and working as domestic servants in a poor but still lovely landscape with hand-stacked stone fences and a quilt made by the God of green all around them. The air was damp and clear and the sea was nearby everywhere you went. There really wasn't an ugly place to look at in their little part of Northern Ireland.

But in 1850, five horrible years of the potato famine had just ended and with it the lives of one million Irish people. Another one million left the island for the Promised Land of North America or at the very least to England to escape death and disease and possibly find something to eat. The poor families that couldn't afford to pay their passage or have a future employer pay it for them, to Canada or America, ended up in England as a last resort, many landing and staying at the port at Liverpool, England. They hoped to return to Ireland when things got better, but for most it did not.[4] Ireland was left with a decimated population of which the McClearys and Hunters were a part.

The poverty and suffering of the Irish people brought on by an insidious mold on their main food crop - the potato - was extreme. The policies of the British government, while initially helpful, were not effective in solving the famine crisis and some commentators claim made the situation far worse. The crops of oats and other food grown in Ireland were still shipped to England (per the laissez-faire thinking of the time) while the Irish people starved. Entire Irish families, unable to pay the rent to their landlord, were expelled from their homes and died homeless at the side of the road, some with green mouths from eating grass to try and stay alive. More Irish men, women and children were filed away in workhouses after surrendering what they had left of their possessions to their landlords. The workhouses included hard work, but it was a building to sleep in out of the weather. Men, women and families were split up and slept in barracks sometimes on the cold, damp stone floor. The workhouses did keep many alive until the worst of the potato famine had passed.

The Irish remaining in Ireland after 1850 had seen starvation, disease, and desperation of epic proportion. The worst of the plight on the potato crop was in the west and southern counties of Ireland so the northern counties may have been less affected, but still suffered a great deal. The North where my family is from was more industrialized than the largely farming Republic and had more varied crops than just the potato to feed its people. The losses in the North were great but not as catastrophic as those in the Republic.[5] The McClearys and Hunters living north of Belfast near Ballymena and the lake called Lough Neagh in the villages and townlands of Clogh, Broughshane, Racavan – all near Slemish Mountain - in 1850 had lived through hell as had all of Ireland. They were poor, traumatized and shell-shocked at what had happened to the people of Ireland in such a short time. But they were still alive and therefore had a chance and some hope.

The story of my people, the Hunters and the McClearys, is one of courage, spirit, sacrifice and humor. They are the resilient and brave people who came to America before me. As in any interesting family, there was treachery, betrayal, tragedy and a goodly amount of secret keeping down through the years. My aunt says some subjects were "Highly Classified" and were never to be spoken of. Out of respect for the dead and fear of the living, I will leave some of the more controversial and painful stories out. This is my tribe and their stories have been rattling around in my head for years wanting to be told: some sad, shocking, inspiring, many funny, all mine. I've carried scraps of paper, napkins, bar mats and journals with facts and notes about my family around with me since 1986. After high school, I began asking questions and trying to understand how we got here, America, and the place we came from, the Old Country. As the pile of papers has grown so has my excitement and urgency to write these stories down to share with my children, other McClearys –and there are lots of us – and even outsiders.

The Hunters and McClearys detested each other. Maybe it started in Ireland, where they lived in close proximity, or picked up its hateful steam later in Scotland around the coal mining villages of Harthill and Blackridge. But the McCleary/Hunter distaste for the other continues to this day. My cousin visited Harthill in the late 70s and the Hunters failed to mention that there were plenty of McClearys in town. My aunt went in 1980 and the same thing, the Hunters assumed she wouldn't want to see a McCleary and on her last day in Harthill she found out there were lots of our people in the village. There was a Hatfield and McCoy-type feud between the Hunters and McClearys about the same time the famous feuders picked up arms in the hillbilly country of the US. Or as one of my old aunts says they were like "the Hatfields and the Martins."

Back in the Old Country, which is what my grandparents called Ireland and Scotland interchangeably, the Hunters were just a little more high class than the McClearys, had a better reputation in the community, and later in Scotland they were managers in the coal mines. They played on sports teams; they worked above ground.[6] The Hunters had it all together and were respected people. The McClearys were outgoing, blue collar, salt-of-the-earth worker folk - still true in my branch of the family today - that made some questionable choices here and there.

McCleary History

In the glens of County Antrim, my great, great grandfather Andrew McCleery (with the double ee) was born in 1856, in the small village of Clogh. The County of Antrim is one of the six counties of Northern Ireland, called Ulster or the North. The largest city in Northern Ireland, Belfast, is in County Antrim. Ulster is both Protestant and Catholic with a Protestant majority and is part of the United Kingdom. The rest of the island of Ireland, south of Ulster is called the Republic of Ireland, or Eire (in Gaelic), or Ireland comprising 26 counties that gained their independence from Britain in the 1920s and are self-governed from Dublin. The Republic of Ireland is mostly Catholic. There is much more to this discussion of religion and boundaries and borders and allegiance to the UK, but I will frame it simply to start.

The village of Clogh is a quaint little place with one road through it; I saw it in 2010 while in Ireland for the first time. Unfortunately the pronunciation of the name, Clogh, involves a lot of phlegm and is not pretty. The surname Andrew features prominently in our family and my dad Jack McCleary, born in 1940, bore a strong resemblance to Andrew

McCleery when they were both wizened old men. Andrew's wife was Betty (also called Betsy and Jane) McVicker, born in 1851 and married Andrew in 1874 when he was 19 and she 20. They were farmers. Great, great grandma Betsy was a true badass; she drove a horse team at seven years of age and sported a club foot all her life from a horse stepping on it. Betsy never went to school, which was probably not that unusual for the time and place, but knew how to run a farm. Andrew (called Andy) played the flute or piccolo in the Orangeman's parade, so he obviously had Protestant (I think Presbyterian) rather than Catholic leanings. The orange in Northern Ireland and on the flag is synonymous with the Unionist cause, or the Protestants that want Ulster to remain a part of the UK. The green on the tricolor Irish flag is for the Republic of Ireland. The Republicans in Ireland want all of Ireland (including N. Ireland) to be free from the UK and united as one country on one island.[7]

My great grandparents were farmers in the townland called Glenleslie. Betsy lived to 92 and Andy to 94: they died in the mid-1940s. In a family photo of the two from the late 1800s, they stand side by side in the doorway of a dark, dank-looking stone cottage in Clogh looking out. Andrew eerily with the same jawline, white hair and mustache of my father 70 years later, Betsy short, round and wide but tough looking, cane in hand. Behind them, barely visible, is a shadowy figure of a tall man – possibly one of their sons. McCleary men are generally tall, well built with light eyes and strong straight noses that usually end up broken in a fight at some point – so then crooked noses.

There are many shared names on both sides of the family tree. Doubles and triples of Roberts, James, Hannahs, Annies, Marys, Lizzies, Andrews, and an overabundance of Janes on both sides – I will try to include nicknames, where I know them. And the spelling of McCleary is treated fast and loose in the Old Country, it started out with the double ee (McCleery) and then morphed into the ea, some say at the Canadian port of entry, others say one of the McCleery children changed it in the Old Country. In records from County Antrim, Ireland in the 1800s, it was sometimes spelled M'Cleery. Another source of confusion is the tradition of naming the eldest son after the paternal grandfather: first and middle name! Then the second male baby after the maternal grandfather, again first and middle name- you get the idea. Then there are those with no middle name at all like my uncle James McCleary, my grandfather James McCleary and his father, well, James McCleary. All without middle names. The name Robert Hunter appears frequently on the family tree; my cousin in Portland, Oregon and another in Washington have this first and middle name today.

These are the stories that were told to me through my life. I am an American woman, mother of two, in my 40s, lifetime resident of the Pacific Northwest. The McCleary stories vary wildly depending on who is telling them. Where there are variations on a theme, I will present them. It is interesting to me how time and memory, paranoia, vanity and regret change the same story retold by different people in the same family through generations. And then there are the embellishers that have told the story so many times that they don't know if it's really true at all, and add on with each retelling. Those stories are rural legends in our case. We never let the truth get in the way of a good story.

My grandfather, James "Pawn" McCleary would tell us cousins, his grandchildren (little urchins then) his stories. All the grandkids (and there were about 30) called our grandpa, Pawn. The eldest grandchild, Linda Downey, couldn't say Grandpa and said Grandpawn, which was shortened to Pawn, so his name ever after was Pawn or Grandpa Pawn. At least to all of the grandkids. We sat a few at a time around his upholstered swivel rocking chair in the 1970s in America – him holding a cup of tea with lots of milk and smoking a Camel no-filter cigarette. Sometimes one of us kids would get to talk and tell a story. We would all butt in at once and struggle to be heard: this gave birth to the quote still alive in the family today, someone yelling, "Who's got the floor?" Storytelling was a tradition, the teller important and it was an honor to have the floor. I just spent some time with my brother and his adult son and they are both damn good storytellers, with the big descriptive lead-in to set the scene followed by the story. Then we look around at each face to see how the story is received. Some families value academics and have Ivy League aspirations for their kids, want them to be legacy students at one of the big east coast schools, we put a high value on storytelling with a good delivery and wit.

Clogh

Betsy and Andy McCleery, my great, great grandparents lived in Clogh which is a tiny - one road through it, life centered around the town pub - place. Clogh is up the road from the village of Broughshane, known as the "Flower Basket of Great Britain" for its beautiful flower festivals. Remember, Northern Ireland is part of the UK and the Republic of Ireland is not. This is all near the bigger town of Ballymena. All of this, the old McCleary-Hunter turf, is north of Belfast, the second largest, and most troubled city in Ireland. The Ireland that I saw in 2010, including Dublin and Belfast, looked as I had always expected it to in my fanciful Irish-American mind. But it was crisper and cleaner with fewer falling down old sod huts than I expected; maybe they were there and I didn't see them as I tore through the countryside next to the Irish Sea on the train. Ireland *is* that green island with craggy outlooks that you see on calendars in America. From above in an airplane, Ireland looks like a handmade blanket of green, all the shades of green, some brown and grey, that someone's grandmother made and would have thrown over a couch. Hand-stacked stone and brambly blackberry bush fences are the curving, misshapen borders between the fields. The time, labor and care taken to make the stacked stone fences, like a very heavy puzzle with light peeking through the cracks, is astounding. Beautiful old stone community churches that I saw in Ireland with the graves coming right up under the windows are very different than America where the cemeteries are set apart, sometimes far across town, from the church. All the graves right there in the churchyard in plain sight seemed much more intimate and respectful to the dead, like the people still held them close.

James McCleery Sr., son of Betsy and Andy, future rat killer and counterfeiter, was born eight miles outside of Clogh on a 40-acre farm in 1876. James had six brothers and sisters, a small family for the time but infant mortality was high and many infants didn't live very long, the gaps in the birth years make me think that they lost a few children. Older children died too, like a son Samuel at age nineteen. They were all born in Clogh or in the near townland called Glenleslie. A townland is a small part of a parish. The children were: Great grandpa James, eldest, born 1876; Elizabeth, born 1879; William, born 1882; Mary, born 1887; Sarah Jane, born 1892; Samuel, born, 1899 and Andrew, born 1901. Most all of great grandpa's siblings would live out their lives and die in Clogh and the area around it. Many of my relatives are buried in the Clogh Graveyard in County Antrim, Northern Ireland. On some of the family headstones, the dead are described as Poor Man, Poor Woman, or Poor Man's son or daughter. It was not an easy life for my ancestors.

James McCleary Sr.'s teen sister Sarah Jane was a flowerer, growing and selling flowers; sister Elizabeth was a linen weaver at age seventeen in the local factories. The linen and lace industry in Northern Ireland and Scotland employed many women and girls in the various mills. Some of the brothers were agricultural laborers around Clogh. The brothers may have been in Gaelic "spailpins" or farm workers that followed work around Ireland as it was available, not really lighting in one place for long. Men and boys in both families, McCleary and Hunter, worked in the mines at Clogh and Broughshane.

The Betsy and Andy McCleary family owned property in Northern Ireland eight miles from Clogh called Laymore Farms on the townland called Tullykittagh. It was a 40-acre working farm with various crops, livestock, poultry – chickens, ducks, geese to sell for food - and a couple of traditional Irish stone cottages. The weather around Laymore Farms was cold, rainy and cloudy most of the time. The old ones in the family spent their time sitting on the bench beside the fire in the cottage to keep the cold and damp off of their feet and legs. In those days when the father died the family holdings went to the eldest brother, or in later times were divided among all the brothers. This tradition went well at Laymore Farms for a couple of generations until there was a nasty fight amongst the brothers over the farm. The eldest brother, James Sr., was on the lam over in Scotland and wasn't there to claim the farm.

A donnybrook (McCleary slang for a big fight) broke out among the other brothers and bad blood ensued. Eventually because of the impasse and stubbornness of the brothers, the farm went on the auction block and one brother bought the farm out from under the other. Then paid it off with the estate money. Treacherous behavior for sure, you should read the old letters. One side brought in lawyers to settle the matter and there was more arguing, controversy and disowning of one another over the family farm. Ultimately it went to the second son, just younger than my great-grandpa, William.

I am not at all surprised to read this in old letters from Laymore because land disputes, bar-fights and infighting are a McCleary family mainstay. The men in the family often turn up with the random, unexplained black eye. By the time I was in third grade, I knew the family fighting vocabulary like my ABCs: a scuffle is a little fight with mild violence and lots of swearing; a donnybrook is a big altercation with cussing, punching and sometimes a fire arm; a free-for-all is like a donnybrook but with more than two people fighting. A rhubarb, was introduced later, and was a tiny fight. Disowning and shunning of family members and friends was common. Sometimes the friend or relative on the receiving end of the shun was never spoken to or acknowledged again.

Growing up it was a little hard to keep track of who was disowned, which included their kids, who you could speak to freely and who you ignored like a stranger. We had a saying, "Look to the left" when passing by someone that the Jack McClearys were pissed off at or avoiding. So the fighting over land generations back doesn't surprise me at all. My dad got crossways with every neighbor we ever had over something or another:

land, behavior of us kids, irrigation, or some injustice that my dad couldn't tolerate. He recommended to us kids, when we were grown, going over to a new neighbor immediately and just telling them to, "Go to hell!" to get it out of the way and establish the no speaking policy to save yourself grief later. Some of the black humor we so enjoy. So let's say the present day McClearys are dramatic and volatile people.

Jane Peacock, my great grandmother was born in the Glens of Antrim area in 1871. The Glens of Antrim is an area of Northern Ireland, also called The Braid since the Braid River runs through it, and is a tourist attraction to this day because of its beauty. On the coast near the Glens is the Giant's Causeway, a natural geologic formation that looks like enormous, uneven, grey LEGO steps out into the sea. Legends abound about giants walking across from Scotland to Ireland on these massive and unusual looking steps. Great grandma Jane is remembered as a sweet lady with Christian tendencies although I don't know if she was a church goer. She married James McCleary, Sr. on November 25, 1898 in Ballymena, County Antrim. Her marriage to James McCleary was a source of conflict in the McCleary clan. Her family held no land so she was considered a poor match for James since the marriage would add nothing to the McCleary Empire. And she was pregnant. James married her and they went to Scotland, forsaking his inheritance of the family farm.

Jane's father was Willie John Peacock and her mother was Mary Morrison. On their marriage certificate from October 21, 1875, Willie John, 28, is a labourer by trade and Mary, 21, recorded as a spinster (weirdly enough). Well young spinster or not, Willie John and Mary were a prolific couple: fifteen children were born of that union, including five sets of twins. I was skeptical about this abnormally high number of twins in one family, because I couldn't see names and dates in the old documents, like the Census, that showed a pack of twins. As it turns out, one child from each set of the five sets of twins died in infancy or youth. Only five of the twins lived into adulthood and thus there were no doubles of birthdates in the records on my grandmother's side. One of great grandma Jane's brothers also called Willie John Peacock, like the father, was a ship's captain and merchant sailor of some renown, and an Orangeman therefore a Protestant. This brother Willie John, master of the seas far and wide, ironically drowned drunk in a shallow canal in Broxburn, Scotland at age 47.

Another family member in this rags to riches story – Thornbirds-like[9] saga, I will introduce now is alcohol: on both sides it plays a central and sometimes starring role through all the generations from these in the 1850s, all the way through to the present in 2012. McClearys, and Hunters for that matter, like to have a drink. My brother and my uncle are brawling, bar-fighting legends in our part of Washington State and a very high percentage of McClearys are alcoholics, both drinking and retired from drinking. We have more than our share of problem drinkers in our family that really shouldn't touch the hooch.

In rural County Antrim, the Hunters and McClearys lived in several parishes and townlands close together. They are Racavan, Clogh, Clogh Mills, Glenleslie and Tullykittagh. Slemish Mountain, which is really more of a biggish hill, sits amongst all these small places and is best known as the place where in old times, around 432 AD Saint Patrick was a slave, a goat-herd, when he was a boy.[10] This was before he went to the Continent and became a Catholic and returned to Ireland to convert the natives to Catholicism and as a side job to drive all the snakes out of Ireland. He also described the Holy Trinity of Father, Son and Holy Spirit by pointing to the three leaves on a green clover, making the clover or shamrock quite famous.

Slemish Mountain is rocky and a bit craggy with flowers and heather sprinkled around. Of course the grass is one of the Irish 40 shades of green and the rocks that you step on while climbing the winding path are mossy and slimy. Sheep graze on the mountain and the view from atop is outstanding, spread out before you like a giant's blanket tossed carelessly down from a bean stalk. The mountain is shaped like a cork sitting on a bed of green and comes from a volcanic plug. Northern Irish families lived in small brick houses or stone cottages with thatched or sod roofs and many took on a family member like an aunt, uncle or cousin to provide a home for and to contribute to the expenses in the home. Northern Ireland was rainy, damp, the work was hard, and life was not easy there for any of the family.

The religious and political unrest in Northern Ireland at this time, 1850-1900, was beginning to heat up between the Protestant minority in the North and the Catholic majority in the south, the Republic of Ireland.[11] My family seemed to come down on the Protestant side although it is said that they emigrated to Scotland specifically to get away from religious fighting. Pawn later said that he and our grandma Jane "Jean" Hunter came to Canada and America to get away from "the religious bullshit" in the Old Country. We have a way with words.

So it seems the McClearys fled the Old Country to get away from religious and political unrest. Not a surprise, the early McClearys in our family were not active churchgoers in America and Pawn was a professed atheist. Later in the United States, parts of the family became churchy, but my dad Jack, not ever. My dad called religious people 'believers' and had nothing against them but did not count himself among them. He worshiped more in the cathedral of nature: the mountains, the rivers, and the ocean of the Pacific Northwest.

Hunter History

Now my grandma's side: The Hunters. My great, great grandfather was William Hunter, and my great, great grandmother was Martha Bones, born in 1851 in County Antrim. Their son, my great grandfather, was the first of the Robert Hunters and in 1904 he married Rachel McAleese in N. Ireland. (Note to self: see if I'm related in some way to Mary McAleese the former President of Ireland.) Rachel's parents were William McAleese and Elizabeth Jane Graham both from County Antrim. The beloved and still talked about Rachel McAleese, my great, great grandmother, was a faith healer in the Old Country. People came from miles around with ailments, especially suffering from gangrene of the feet and toes, and she would heal them with the power of God. Her method to administer this power was a bread poultice that she made by pouring boiling water on a piece of bread and applying that to the wound. Rachel was on the Hunter side, which was the more mainstream and conservative of the two bloodlines that I come from, but she was unconventional with her faith healing and alternative medicine.

My grandmother Jane "Jean" Hunter (everyone had a nickname, or two) was born in County Antrim on farm at the base of Slemish Mountain near the village of Broughshane in 1905. My Grandma Jean was the eldest of ten children, there were eleven - but one, Anna, died shortly after birth. The Hunter children were all girls except for the baby boy Robert who it is said was a spoiled brat. Laundry list of the girls: my Grandma Jean, Elizabeth "Lizzie," Martha, Sarah, Rachel, Jenny, Kathy, Mary, Rosetta "Nettie," all born between 1905 and 1920. My Grandma Jean was a strong and capable woman, although she was small, 5'4", and petite; she must have gotten her early training overseeing this crew as the eldest child. She would later have her own crew to contend with in Scotland, Canada and America. Grandma Jean was very close with the sister just younger than her, Aunt Lizzie. There were very close in age, what some call Irish twins.

Pawn was the third born of twelve kids in his family, the oldest born in the Clogh, County Antrim area and some born in Harthill, Scotland and more again around Clogh, N. Ireland. There was lots of back and forth between Scotland and Ireland during these birthing years, following work in the mines. Pawn remembered and talked about sailing across the North Channel, between the two countries when he was a small boy, he said three years old. Around 1900, the mining industry in Northern Ireland had gone into decline and by 1919 there was hardly any mining at all because of the lack of explosives due to World War I.[12] The distance from where the two families (McCleary and Hunter) lived in Broughshane, County Antrim to the coalfields in Scotland is not far, about 150 miles as a crow flies to the northeast on the other side of the North Channel above the Irish Sea. This dozen McCleary children were from old to young: Nan born out of wedlock in 1897, Andrew, Elizabeth, William, James (Pawn), Sam, Jeannie, John, Hannah and Mary, Anna, and finally Robert born in 1914. The baby John died at eleven months old from a concussion by falling out of bed onto a stone floor. The twins Hannah and Mary were born the day the Titanic, built in Belfast, went down in the Atlantic Ocean: that's the way my grandpa remembered it.

I interviewed my grandfather in 1986 and got all this information straight from the horse's mouth, as it were. I lived in Boise, Idaho, at nineteen and thought I should document some of the family history from the fabled Old Country. Pawn died a year or so later. When our grandpa died at age 82 he had seven living kids, 43 grandkids, and 28 great grand kids. Now of course in 2012, there are even more of us having bred all over the place, especially in eastern Washington State where the bulk of the James McCleary people still live. We are good breeders, it seems. I am related to half of the town of Richland, Washington. In this story I call my grandfather Pawn because that was his name to me and all of his grandkids. But the nickname Pawn is interesting. Was he a pawn from Scotland for the UK sent to populate Canada, enticed with a much cheaper ticket than coming in to Ellis Island? On his immigration papers is says he was bound for Edmonton, Alberta to be a farmer travelling on the Colonization Program. Was he a pawn for an international labor union spreading the word in America to workers in Butte, Montana and Richland, Washington?

In my grandpa's family, his sister Nan (the eldest) is credited with changing the spelling of the family name McCleery. Pawn told me there was a nursery rhyme that went "1-2-3 O'Leery fall down on your bumble-eery" and his sister Nan hated it and the school kids teased her like hell so she had the whole family change to McCleary. I am not sure if a little kid wielded this sort of power, but probably so. The parents were too busy

15

trying to keep the kids alive and not falling out of beds in those difficult days to care about spelling and semantics. Incidentally, the ancient meaning of McCleary is "the cleric" or writer of the village. The Mc prefix means Son of … in the Gaelic language. McClearys have been called 'son of a' lot of things through the years, but rarely the cleric.

Robert Hunter in Racavan, County Antrim, Northern Ireland, age 12 1893

Above: Andrew and Betsy McCleary, Clogh, County Antrim, N. Ireland. 1916 Below: James McCleary Sr. (2nd from left, seated) and siblings. Clogh, County Antrim, N. Ireland. 1920

CHAPTER 3

HARTHILL, SCOTLAND - 1900

The McClearys and the Hunters followed the work from their homeland in Broughshane, Antrim to the Harthill, Scotland area. The Harthill, Blackridge, and Shotts area is on the road between Glasgow and Edinburgh near the River Almond. I heard my grandpa say many times that he was from a town "halfway between Edinburgh and Glasgow." The work available in the Harthill, Blackridge, Shotts communities was drift coal mining. Drift mining is described as a mine tunnel that follows the direction or "drift" of a vein.[13] According to the Scottish Mining website, in 1900-10 there were 23 mines in Scotland. The men went ahead from Ireland to Scotland and secured work in the mines then sent for the families to come.

The McClearys – fourteen of them - lived in the miners housing at 63 and later 66 Victoria Street and on Westrigg Road, dismal, stone row houses, dark and damp or outright wet with hard flagstone floors. The majority of the miners and their families lived in the miners' rows that were rented by the Company to the masses of people living in Harthill and the surrounding villages. The Hunters (Grandma Jean's family) because of their management status in the mines lived in the better quality two-story housing with private toilet facilities and even a little yard at Baird Terrace. The Terrace homes and the Westrigg and Victoria St. row houses were in close proximity but in reality a world apart.

Due to the influx of mine workers and overcrowding in the Scottish mining towns in the early 1900s, many of the families in the row houses took in lodgers. Between twelve and nineteen people between the family and the lodgers sometimes lived in the three room dwellings, with two rooms below and a low attic above. The women and girls in these homes cooked and cleaned and served the men on each shift. When a woman married a miner, the contract was that they would support the miner and his work, period. They prepared basic food: porridge, tea and scones, jam and bread, once in a while stews with cheap cuts of meat. The young girls in the families made the lunches for the workers and packed them in their pieceboxes. They were made of heavy metal that no rat or mouse could breach, with a handle to carry. A separate metal container with one side for tea and one for sugar carried their drink. The miners worked in shifts: day, back, and night and the beds in the row housing were occupied in shifts by different people throughout the day. When a miner stumbled home exhausted from the mine, or drunk from the after work pub, he fell into a still warm bed since someone had just got up to go to work. Privacy was nonexistent.

There were two outhouses the miners' rows for 150 men. The women had to fend for themselves somehow and the children just relieved themselves beside the rows. There was an old man employed by the mine owner to wander the miners housing and clean up, scrape up after the children with a shovel. Possibly a worse job than a rat killer. Running water was available at two spouts in the dirt road if you were lucky. Often one wall of the row house was damp and rotted from moisture, rats were everywhere and clothes washed outside of the cheap brick housing blocks. The dwellings only had a front door, no back door, so to get behind you had to walk the length of the row, usually 33 houses. The lodgers had to pay quite a high rent to the mine owners, or other landlords for these poor housing conditions. The families shopped in the company store or the Co-Operative it was called, the only shop available, and bought staples at elevated prices.

Rat Killer

So, James McCleary, Sr. was a rat killer or a ratter they called it. He was a thin, wiry man with a sour, smart-ass expression, and mischievous sparkly eyes. He was small, spunky and full of life. He ran down rats in the dark low tunnels below ground and exterminated them. Killing techniques at the time were whacking the rats with eighteen inches of rubber hose, sending in a couple ferrets or a Yorkshire terrier to track and kill them.[14]

The ferrets were particularly vicious and hunted in pairs and took great zeal in tearing their prey to pieces. In the Scottish coal mines the hose of death was the preferred tool because it was cheap and didn't require care like the ferrets and dogs did.[15] The brown rats, with little heads and large arses, as the miners said, came down into the mine with the grain and oats for the ponies.

The pit ponies, as they were called, that pulled the coal cars up and out of the mine were mostly ponies from Norway and spent all of their lives, 20 years or so, underground working those tunnels. The ponies and the fourteen year old boys that usually cared for them and lead them in the dark, the pony drivers, were about the same height. Some of the ponies were crafty and opened the pieceboxes to eat the miners' cheese or jam sandwiches. Some say that the ponies were so smart that they could uncork a bottle of booze and drink that too; I'm not sure about that fact. At times, as many as 35 ponies or horses would work in one pit at a time. Some of the animals were Shetland ponies and were stabled underground, only coming out of the mine once a year at holiday time when the mine closed briefly. They had to be four years old to work as a pit pony in the mine; a lifetime in the darkness and trudging the same tunnels in the coal mine. They pulled the heavy carts full of coal led by a boy, but after a while they knew the way out and the boy keeping track of the cart would ride on the cart rather than leading the animal. The men and boys that cared for the ponies became very attached to the animals and shared their food with them.

The rats, attracted to the ponies' food, multiplied quickly once they got down there and became aggressive and vicious when they couldn't find anything to eat. The men kept their cheese sandwich or jam sandwich and tea and sugar only in metal containers for this reason. Mine rats were known to steal an entire metal lunch container. Now that I'd like to see. The rats were not only a nuisance but caused a hazard to the workers. One shift manager was chasing a rat out of the work area and got mowed down and killed by one of the metal coal carts that ran haphazardly on the rails all over the mines.[16] The cars weighed up to a ton when loaded with coal. Many times in the tunnels the coal carts careened out of control and jumped the tracks. You could hear the high-pitched shrieking of the boys trying to gain control of the load and the pony in the tunnels. You knew it was a boy pony driver, no man had a voice that high. The rats also peed on lunches and in the underground streams in the mine and the men would get sick if they came in contact with the urine. So James McCleary Sr.'s job was to kill them and haul them out.

While the rats were a problem in too great a number, they were nice to have as an alarm system. Miners in the UK and America relied on the dirty devils to let them know when a cave-in was coming. The theory is, the rats could sense the movement and shifting in the mine that preceded a disaster and would all charge out a day or so before it happened. In some of the accounts from Scotland and Wales hundreds would run out in one swarm. The miners trusted and relied on this signal and laid down their tools and followed the rats out. Invariably a day or so later something would give way and scores of miners would have been killed. Like taking a canary in a mine to see if it died from the toxic gases, the rats would signal imminent danger. The miners knew they were safe if the rats were rooting around peacefully and not agitated. Agitated rats equaled scared and jumpy men.[17] Some were friendly with the rats, they weren't afraid of people and were very bold. Some workers would hold them on their laps and give them pieces of food at break time when they were having a smoke a mile or two down.

Working in a Scottish coal mine in 1900-1925 was backbreaking work, literally. The men and boys that worked down there were in tunnels sometimes only four feet high, in absolute darkness except for lanterns and head lamps, and stifling heat doing difficult and dangerous work. There are accident reports from the mines and a man or boy was killed about every other day amongst all the mines in the area, about 23 working mines in the 1920s. Many deaths were from falls down the shaft (some drunk but mostly sober), or explosions, or rock cave-ins, or accidents with the machines used in and around the mine. All through the 1800s there were women and children under thirteen working in the mines until the law passed that they could only work above ground around the mouth of the mine or the face. So just the mature, seasoned old men of fourteen could mine for coal after that.

So the women miners, many widows, who couldn't find work anywhere else, kept the railway of coal cars going back and forth and did tough, heavy mechanical work. When a new miner came on the job the women in the dirty shawls and unusually short skirts, which were formerly nice old dresses now tied up around their legs with string, craned their necks to look and see if he was a possible husband. Anything to take them away from the work at the face of the mine and back to respectability. Because of the men dying in the mines so frequently, many former housewives had to do whatever work they could to keep the families alive. Girls in the village at thirteen, finished the school year and came to work with the older women at the face and for many that was their career for life.

In accident reports from the time, the frequency of deaths is shocking – sometimes one every day in at least one of the mines. For example, there is a story about a boy who worked at the mouth of the mine. He was with a group of lads, bored, waiting around for work, playing with a ball on and around a huge piece of machinery. The fourteen year old fell in the machine, was horribly mangled and died. This was not unusual at all.

Boys started down inside the mine as pony drivers at fourteen. Some were nippers, fetching tools for the workers or manning the doors that helped contain toxic gases or fire in the miles of different tunnels. Boredom was a problem for the nippers so they played with rats to pass the time, trapping them and such. Little boys and girls called pickers worked sorting out the coal, some were only five or six years old working a ten-hour day while sitting up on a metal conveyor belt wearing rags for clothes with bare feet. Many miners that survived their working years in the pits would come down with respiratory illnesses that killed them in old age. This is very common across the mining industry around the world.

James Sr. eventually worked his way up and retired as a brusher at one of the mines in Harthill. Brusher was the most physically difficult job underground: you were breaking trail into new tunnels, picking out the rock and sending it out of the mine. A hewer also dug coal in the pit; a mucker cleaned up waste rock with a shovel; a drawer filled the hutches (carts) and moved them to a central point. The excellent job of faceman, managing the men, was above ground at the mine's mouth. Coal bearers carried coal out on their backs and putters pushed the heavy coal carts out of the mine; before the labor laws of the early 1900s these jobs were for kids and women. Women and children bagged the coal up at the mine face well into the 20th century.[18]

But between rat killer and brusher in the mine, James McCleary Sr. was a counterfeiter, as well as a cobbler. The criminal conviction for counterfeiting would cause a wealth of problems later on for James Sr. and the whole family. Oh and my grandpa said James Sr. was a drinker. My grandpa, with James Sr. for a father, had a strict home life with his 11 brothers and sisters in the Harthill miners' rows. James Sr. did not allow his children to sit at the family table to eat, they each had to stand until they brought home their first paycheck for the family at age 14 and handed it to mother. Only then would father nod and they could sit in a chair to eat for the first time in their lives. This was true for the boys as well as the girls; the McCleary girls were weavers in the linen or lace mills or domestic servants. James Sr. didn't acknowledge his children in public whether they were young or adults. He walked on by as if he didn't know them.

Thankfully, my great grandmother Jane Peacock McCleary was a gentle and sweet woman. She had soft, friendly features and wore delicate wire rimmed glasses. Pawn talked about his mother with fondness and said she was a good Christian woman and lived by those principles. Pawn took after her even though he never considered himself religious, the only draconian stunts he pulled were pickiness about how to cut the sharp cheddar with the wire cheese cutter and allowing his kids 1 inch water, max in the bathtub per child per bath. Pawn was hard on the boys in the family and favored the girls, same as my dad - much to the chagrin of my three brothers. I think favoring daughters is an Irish dad trait, I've heard as much from other Irish and Irish Americans. In the Old Country pictures you see James Sr. with the bright eyes hanging on and palling around with his daughters when they were grown up and had families of their own.

The rite of passage for both a miner and a man was on their fourteenth birthday, they went from wearing the short pants or knickers of a boy to wearing the long pants of a man. This change in legwear signaled the end of childhood (such as it was, with all that standing) and the beginning of manhood and mine work. Pawn was among the four eldest boys and he with brothers Andrew, William and Sam each finished eighth grade and started work at the mines near Harthill at age fourteen. The boys went from holding a ball and stick to holding a heavy piecebox in the matter of one day.

Pawn, fifteen, and his three brothers, aged fourteen, eighteen and twenty walked the seven miles together to work from the village Harthill. The cage lowered them down the mine shaft anywhere up to two miles down and Pawn army-crawled for one to two miles in a confined tunnel to his work station each day, and of course crawled out after working fourteen hours. All the coal he'd shoveled for the day was in a lorry that he had to push out ahead of him to the lift station. Pawn joined the labor union (United Mineworkers) and worked in the coal mines around Harthill steadily from eighth grade to age 23.

To keep somewhat sane in the depths of the coal mine, the miners sang. In the winding tunnels you would hear a popular song of the day belted out and another crew would join in and keep the song going. Especially lively was the singing when the shift was over and they were waiting for the cage to take them back up to the surface. The men loved to sing and some sang very well. There were deep tenor Pavarotti voices and high voices of the young, and everything in between. Pawn sang all through his life and taught his kids to enjoy singing, whether they sang well or not.

Between 1910 and 1912, Andrew, Pawn's oldest brother, who was born and went to school in Clogh, County Antrim, N. Ireland - began saving money for a touring bicycle and a big adventure. It was hardship enough to save money to buy the bike; most of the money he made in the mine went to their mother and they only made 50 cents a week. Uncle Andy managed to purchase a fancy bicycle, lightweight and state of the art, and at age fifteen headed out to see his school chums in Northern Ireland. Andy, so proud and excited to own such a bike and go on this journey alone, crossed the North Channel on the ferry and rode through Belfast toward the hill country in Antrim. Along this route he got caught in the middle of a Unionist (Protestant) mob fighting a Republican (Catholic) mob. Each side saw the kid and assumed he was a spy for the other side. Uncle Andy was severely beaten and left for dead alongside the road in Northern Ireland. His treasured bike was badly mangled and so was he. Someone found him and took him to the hospital where he was in a coma for two months. Andy never fully recovered from this attack. The beating that almost killed Uncle Andy tainted my grandfather against the Irish and Ireland at large.

Pawn was born in Scotland and after the beating of his brother he aligned himself with the Scottish (he called Scotch) people much more than the Irish, though that is his ancestral homeland. Pawn bitterly that Irish men were drunks and wife beaters and he never went back to Ireland. The beating in Belfast was part of the "religious bullshit" that he wanted to get away from and that drove him to Canada and the U.S. In America, Pawn was called Scotty and Old Scotty by friends and that was the way he preferred to be known. Grandma Jean didn't share this sentiment and went back to Ireland a few times, remarking on a postcard of Slemish Mountain sent to my other grandparents, the Rawlings in Richland: "Hi Jane and Bud, Do hope this finds both of you in the best- I am sending you a picture of where I was born at the foot of this Hill. Had a nice time in Ireland - like it much better than Scotland... Cheerio, Love Jean and Jim"

The Hunters lived a very different life in Harthill than the McClearys. My great grandpa Robert Hunter was a dapper, pulled together man born in Racavan, County Antrim, near Slemish Mt. in 1882. He especially hated the McClearys and did not want his eldest daughter Jane "Jean" to get involved with one. In the collieries of Scotland the Hunters ascended into management positions and worked above ground managing scores of men underground. Hunters played on the local sports teams like the Westrigg Rovers football club and were well adjusted contributors to the community. The Hunters weren't rich by any means: my grandmother Jean Hunter lived and worked in Edinburgh at the Royal Infirmary as a nurse's assistant in her teens. She was a candy striper as we would say in America. She also had etiquette training and learned the rituals of formal dining, place settings and such that would serve her well. My grandma spoke Gaelic and did so with the patients there as well as learned sign language to communicate with the deaf in the hospital. Much later in America she would talk in sign with people that she met that were deaf. The Hunters lived in the Terraces in Harthill and the Terrace dwellers didn't mix with the folk in the miners' rows. Well, most of them didn't.

My grandpa traveled around Scotland with a troupe of prize fighters to take on local tough guys in what they called a smoker. He fought for food or for money to save for America, since his coal mine earnings still went to his mother for the family. Pawn wasn't a big man, a thin 5' 10", but exceedingly strong and sinewy - he had the punching power to knock men out cold in the 250 lb. and up range, according to his youngest son Howard. They conducted the matches on the border between two counties, because it was illegal and when police approached from either side the boxers would escape into the other county. As I remember, Pawn's arms looked like those on a Canova sculpture that I saw in the Borghese Gallery in Rome - but with freckles.

Growing up in Scotland, Pawn had lots of guy chums. He was charismatic and handsome with sparkly blue eyes, light hair and attracted friends easily. They just happened to have great names and nicknames: Gigi McAllister, Toffee Boner, Leeky McMackin, and Horsey Shaw. My grandpa was the dud with just plain old Jim McCleary for a name - that would change in time. In these years he was out with his friends around Scotland, dressed very spiffy and having a good time. In some of the old photos the guys are arm in arm walking on a boardwalk that looks like a Scottish version of Atlantic City. Many of these families working in Harthill had lived in the Clogh area of County Antrim as well. Harthill, Blackridge, and Shotts were full of transplants from the hill country of County Antrim.

Pawn and Grandma Jean each attended school until the eighth grade, where they met and got to know each other and later fell in love. Jean's father Robert Hunter was furious and railed against a McCleary seeing his daughter or God forbid, coming into his family. He knew the father James Sr. and his record of achievements and assumed the sons were the same: rat killers, common crooks, and drunks. James (Pawn) McCleary and Jean Hunter married in 1927 in Scotland. I wish I knew more about their courtship but Grandma Jean, while she talked and chatted over many cups of tea and while serving many customers in restaurants, never revealed much personal information about her life. A couple of my aunts told me this about their mother…

Weddings in the mining villages of Scotland in the 1920s were simple gatherings to get the job done. The couple, her in a simple dress and he in a suit if he had one, was married in the family home, they signed the documents right there and walked out man and wife. Not a lot of hoopla. It was understood that the wife's duty was to support the man with food preparing, home keeping, kid keeping, so he could work in the mine and keep them all in a house and provide the food. The Hunters were not at all pleased when their oldest daughter Jean married the younger James McCleary. The father, Robert Hunter felt this was setting a bad precedent - to have the oldest of his eight daughters fall in with a family such as the McClearys.

Where weddings were quick and straightforward, funerals were a more emotional affair in the villages around the coal mines. When someone died, which was often, they had what they called a chesting. A chesting consisted of the minister coming to the home of the deceased, where they were laid out in funeral clothes, and saying a few words of comfort. Then the undertaker would drag in the austere wooden coffin. Someone in the family, usually the mother of the deceased, would put the prepared body in the coffin. If it was a child the mother would place him or her in the coffin herself and then kiss the child to say goodbye. If it was an adult, a couple of people would help to get the body in the casket. The chesting part was the undertaker putting the wooden lid on and clamping it down and slowly bolting it closed. This part was the final goodbye to the loved one and wailing and crying would commence when the lid was secured on the chest or coffin.

In Harthill, Shotts Parish, Scotland, my grandparents had their first child on June 6, 1928, another James McCleary: my Uncle Jim. At the time of Jim's birth, Pawn was a coal miner and Jean was a domestic servant. Pawn was getting good and sick of working in the mine since he had been down in there since age 14 and said "to hell with this; we're going to North America." He didn't want to raise his children to work in the mines like him or be domestic servants for rich families in Scotland or Ireland. Grandma Jean was close with her mother Rachel McAleese Hunter and the McCleary house was not as welcoming to her and her baby. Jane Peacock probably wanted to see her grandson but with James Sr. on a drunk of some sort or stamping out money it would have been difficult. In those days in Scotland and Northern Ireland, and all of the UK, the late 1920s, you had to travel with a quota. My aunt told me it was a travel pass that you got once in your life, if you didn't travel "when your quota came up" you never got another chance. Whether or not that is true, it is what they believed.

In June 1928, when Uncle Jim was ten days old my grandfather's quota to sail to North America came up. Emigrants leaving Scotland were strongly encouraged to go to Canada rather than America because Britain through its Colonization Department wanted to populate Canada, one of its possessions. Pawn along with hundred other young, strong Scotsmen had attended a job fair put on locally by UK officials to recruit fit, young workers to emigrate to Canada to be farmers. Pawn had never farmed but something other than mining, anything but mining, was exciting and appealing especially in Canada. Ship fare to Canada was cheaper than to New York or any port on the east coast of the United States. Pawn was one of the first of the family to come to North America. His brother Andrew, that got beat up in Belfast, came before him through Ellis Island at New York City. Uncle Andy worked as a laborer building the railroad in Pennsylvania and later settled in Michigan on a fruit farm. Uncle Andy changed the spelling – or someone changed it for him – of McCleary to MacCleary when he entered the USA. In later years Pawn's sister Lizzie and brother Sam came to Canada and lived there the rest of their lives.

Pawn at age 23 had mentally prepared himself to leave where he had grown up and all he knew and would send for Jean and the baby when he was settled in Canada and their quotas came through. He didn't know if he'd see his parents and siblings ever again. He was headed for Edmonton, Alberta, to work as a farmer in the Colonization Program. His ship, a Canadian Pacific Line vessel called CVM Montclare sailed on June 17, 1928, from the dock at The Tail of the Bank, near Greenock, Scotland. Between 1926 and 1928 about 150 people per ship sailed out of The Tail of the Bank to work in Canada: the Cunard Line and Canadian Pacific picked up there. The emigrants were Scottish from the North and South, many signed on as farmers, but also ironworkers and or domestics.

The ship's route was from the west coast of Scotland across the North Channel above the Irish Sea into the Atlantic Ocean and west to Montreal, Quebec, in Canada. Pawn called it Immigrant Ship #2424 and always said he had to pay $17 dollars upon his arrival at the Canadian port. The Montclare had two masts, two funnels and weighed 16,000 tons.[19] Pawn sent a postcard back to Jean in Scotland with the ship Montclare on it and on the back he conveyed his sadness at having to leave his wife and new baby so soon after Jim's birth. He told Grandma Jean that he hoped she was doing better than when he left and was not so upset. It was not easy for

Pawn to leave his wife and ten day old son behind. But the prospect of raising his family in squalor in the Scottish mining towns was unthinkable.

In August 1928, when Uncle Jim was two months old Grandma Jean's quota came up. But no quota for the baby. My grandmother had to decide what to do, use the quota and follow Pawn - leaving her first-born child briefly behind or stay in Scotland and never get another chance to go to Canada or America since the quota was a one-time opportunity. It was common knowledge that if your quota came up and you didn't use it you never got another. Jean had her photograph taken for the passport when Pawn got his, so she had that in hand. My Grandma Jean sailed to Canada on an Italian vessel called the Andania on August 20, 1928.[20] Uncle Jim (the baby) was two months old and stayed behind in Scotland with his grandmother, Jean's mother Rachel McAleese (the faith healer). They would send for him right away when they got the money together in Canada and somehow arranged for his expedited quota.

Robert Hunter, Harthill, Scotland -around 1940

Jean Hunter, job @
Royal Infirmary,
Edinburgh,
Scotland. 1921
(Front row, left)

Right:
Hunter relatives on
the Miners Row,
50 Victoria St.,
Harthill, Scotland
On back, says
"bitch of a
woman"

James McCleary
Sr. w/ twins
Hannah & Mary,
Anna.
(above)

James and
Hannah (right)
Harthill, Scotland

All 1940s

James "Pawn"
McCleary (left),
14

His brother,
Samuel
McCleary,
13

1918
Harthill,
Scotland.

Brother, Andrew
McCleary, 20

Mother, Jane
Peacock
McCleary

Harthill,
Scotland
1918

Jane "Jean" Hunter, 22

James "Pawn" McCleary, 22

Passport photos, 1929 Harthill, Scotland

James (Pawn) McCleary's ship to N. America the Montclare, 1928 (above)

James "Uncle Jim" McCleary in Royal Air Force Scotland, Age 15 WWII 1943 (left)

CHAPTER 4

MONTREAL, QUEBEC CANADA - 1928

Grandma Jean's ship steamed into Montreal in the Canadian Province of Quebec and she could scarcely believe that the ten days at sea crossing the Atlantic were over and she was in North America. The conditions on the ship were decent: she had a berth, a blanket, mattress and a bolster. The Cunard Line that ran the steamship provided three meals a day, plenty of water and free medical care on the ship. [21] The third class quarters were crowded with immigrants from all over Europe heading to Canada or going on to America on their own from Montreal.

The conditions on immigrant ships in the late 1920s were far and away better than the ships that sailed the Atlantic in the 1840s and 1850s, called the coffin ships. Those ships were horrendous with sickness, disease, vermin and many of the immigrants fleeing the potato famine died on board and were tossed into the sea. Many more famine survivors died on board waiting at the port in North America. Jean's ship the Andania from the Cunard line, an Italian vessel, was clean and held up well through rough seas and fog. But having only crossed the North Channel from Ireland to Scotland before, the travel across the Atlantic was new and frightening to Jean, but far worse than that was the emotional pain of leaving her newborn baby Jim behind. This to the 23 year old, first-time mother Jean, was almost unbearable. The further the ship sailed west the more her heart broke. How many times on the trip did she wish she had never left him and could go back to Scotland where she had lived since she was a girl fresh from Northern Ireland, that she could sail back to her baby. Jim was

35

waiting for her in Montreal, but was he worth it? Should she have just stayed put with her baby in Harthill and let him go ahead with his life in North America? He was a McCleary after all, and her father had been so against it. But Jim was not like his father, James Sr., at all. He was the opposite. Where James Sr. was a drunk and a cheat, breaking the law and getting caught, and mean as the devil-bad as poison, Jim was sweet and ambitious and honest. Grandma Jean was sure they could somehow get a quota for the baby and bring him right away and would all be together again. At least baby James was with her mother and would get good care, but that was little consolation. Still the pain of leaving her baby Jim was gut-wrenching and made her physically sick – far worse than the pitching ship bobbing its way like a black and white cork across the sea.

Jane "Jean" Hunter McCleary came to shore in Montreal on August 30, 1928, and sent her sister a postcard saying "the voyage was splendid." On the ship manifest she is listed as Jane Hunter and had a job arranged as a domestic servant for a Mr. H.E. Guppy of the Wholesale Grocers outfit in Windsor, Ontario. Jean had this position set up through her family and their connections in Harthill, because Windsor, Ontario was a pocket of Scottish immigrants in Canada at that time. Mr. Guppy paid her fare and for travel to his farm and home. Pawn hitchhiked to Windsor, Ontario from Edmonton, Alberta and joined my grandma there. Jean was a domestic servant or nanny for the Guppys, a rich and respected family with a luxury Tudor Revival home and a sizable farm to supply their grocery empire in Canada. Pawn worked for the family as a hired hand outside on the farm. The large Guppy home still stands in Windsor today as a historic register site.[22] The house was new when my grandma arrived and on the fanciest street in Windsor. Compared to the miners housing in the coalfields of Scotland this home and farm was incredible to Jean and Pawn. They were put up in servants' quarters more luxurious than any home they had known. The family was good to Jim and Jean; they treated them like family while they worked at the Guppy house and farm.

In Windsor, Canada working for the Guppys, Jean got pregnant with her second child, which was distressing since her first was not with her yet. My aunt, Betty Rachel (named after Jean's mother Rachel), was born April 17, 1930. Betty was a perfect, beautiful baby and everyone loved her. The wealthy owners of the farm liked Jim and Jean, grew extraordinarily fond of Betty and asked Pawn and Grandma Jean if they could buy her and keep her. Pawn famously said, "Christ man, I'm not going to sell you my baby!" My Aunt Betty as an old woman thought this was funny and seemed so proud that her dad didn't sell her off. Her passport photo from shortly after this does show what a darling and cherubic infant that she was -

36

certainly worthy of purchasing. Shortly after this incident, Pawn crossed the border into America at the Detroit border crossing to see what he could find for the McClearys there.

Brothers: from left to right, Andy, James, Sam, Willie McCleary in Canada. Below: Betty McCleary's Canadian passport, 1930

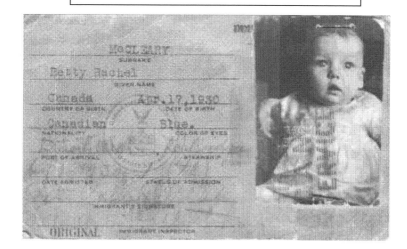

CHAPTER 5

DETROIT, MICHIGAN USA - 1930

In 1930s America the Great Depression was on and Pawn was walking, literally, right into the middle of it. My grandpa crossed into the United States of America for the first time from Canada at Detroit, Michigan, on January 21, 1930. He found odd jobs and worked for ten months. Pawn then sent for Grandma Jean and baby Betty, and they arrived on October 16, 1930. Detroit is just over the river from Windsor, Ontario. Pawn worked in Detroit and times were hard; they were for everyone. Pawn's older brother Andy was living in Michigan on a fruit farm and Jean and Pawn and the baby stayed with him.

Back in 1923, after James Sr. served his time for the counterfeiting felony, his reputation was in tatters and he made a run for Canada. His wife Jane and the twelve kids stayed behind in Harthill. He marked on the form that he had no intention of returning to his family. James boarded a steamer near Greenock, Scotland, steamed across the Atlantic for ten days but ran into trouble at the port trying to enter Canada. Word of his criminal conviction in Scotland had reached Canada just ahead of him and the Canadian border officials turned him away. His only choice was to reboard another ship immediately for Scotland or Ireland, somewhere in the Old Country, and sail back. The forms filled out by the Canadians at the border said, in their estimation, that James McCleary would become a drain on Canadian society and he was denied admittance. James Sr. was 45.

Not easily rebuked, James Sr. tried to get into North America again, this time in 1929 when he was 52. The voyage was the same: long, rough seas, crowded in third class or steerage on the Cunard Line ship Antonia. But this time James Sr. had a new strategy. He brought along the missus, and six of his kids. The little one came: Robert, 11, the twins Hannah and Mary, 17, Annie, 18 and two of the older kids, Jean, 21 and William, 24. How could anyone turn away a family man *and* his family looking for a better life? So he marked on the paperwork that he was not and never had been a felon. They were travelling on the program called The Land Settlement Scheme to Toronto, Ontario and the girls were committed as domestics and the boys farmers in Canada, the youngest Robert would remain a scholar. The children were quite frightened having never traveled by sea anywhere.

At the port in Montreal, Quebec, they a waited to go through the immigration line into Canada. A gruff, harried official looked over the documents of the two elder McCleary kids and passed them through. When he got to James McCleary Sr.'s passport and papers he stopped and frowned. "Didn't you try to enter Canada back in 1923?" James nodded yes. "Why are you back again? Aren't you a felon?" After Jim's explaining and spinning quite a story, the official stamped his papers, DENIED. Again, Canada thought he'd be a drain on good Canadian society and this time added that he suffered from moral turpitude, that his crime in the Old Country was especially dishonest and vile. Unfortunately this ruling meant that his wife and minor children were denied and deported too. The two eldest got to stay, but the rest were shipped back after being held at the port for a week or more.

Detained and Deported was a shameful thing to happen to a family, and everyone knew it. Back they went on another ship the Andania, to Scotland. The twins Hannah and Mary deported with the rest. They were born on the day the Titanic went down, also a Cunard Line ship. The teen girls were uneasy with one trans-Atlantic trip on a Cunard ship; two trips on two different Cunard ships was a nightmare. They were well aware of the fate of another Cunard Line ship, the Titanic. It was a long, sad trip back to the Old Country and to their same, ordinary lives. They felt defeated, cheated and James Sr. was angry. James Sr. never did make it to Canada or the United States.

With the apparent luck of the Irish, 24 year old, Jean McCleary found work as a domestic servant at Henry Ford's mansion called Fair Lane outside of Detroit in Dearborn, Michigan. Henry Ford, the great industrialist and inventor of the Model T and the auto production line, lived on this estate with his wife Clara. The estate was named after the village that Mr. Ford's father and grandfather came from in County Cork, Ireland. Of course, the Fair Lane would also become a popular Ford car. This mansion was even grander than the Guppy home in Windsor and Fair Lane was much larger. 58 rooms! Jean was flabbergasted at the wealth of the Fords and the elegance of this home, like a castle. The Fords only had one child, Edsel.

The Fair Lane mansion is 31,000 square feet and sits on 1300 acres with manicured lawns. The landscape was designed by landscape architect Jens Jensen with all kinds of different gardens that Mrs. Ford requested, like the Blue Garden, the English Rose Garden with 12,000 rose bushes, and other sumptuous themed gardens. Fair Lane did look just like a castle and was designed that way after the Fords made their first trip to Europe and were inspired by real castles there. The Rouge River ran right beside it. An early design for Fair Lane was done by architect Frank Lloyd Wright, in his sparse prairie style, but he was let go from the job when he ran off to Europe with one of his other clients.[23] Plenty of maids, some Irish and Scottish, buzzed about the house and she fit right in. Henry Ford's father, an Irish immigrant from County Cork, came to America in the Famine years, 1845-50. Like the McClearys, the early Fords were immigrants that came to the New World with nothing.[24]

Grandma Jean mingled easily with the rich, powerful and famous. Jean had a way of talking with and endearing herself to people in positions of authority. Maybe it was the Irish charm, the blue eyes, the sharp wit, the strong work ethic. Thomas Edison and his wife were close friends of the Fords and frequent overnight guests at Fair Lane around this time. Grandma Jean had to ride the city bus from Detroit out to the mansion each day to work and back, some of the help lived on the property in servants' cottages but not the maids.[25] My grandfather took care of baby Betty while Jean worked during the day and he worked at night doing whatever work he could find. They were in America at last, but it wasn't the land of milk and honey that they had hoped for. It was just as hard as the Old Country, but it held the promise of something better.

From Detroit, Pawn was in touch via letters and postcards with his friends in Harthill, Blackridge and Bathgate, Scotland: Gigi, Toffee, Leeky, Horsey and Davey Blue. His buddy Archie McCafferty had come to America and was working out west in Butte, Montana with his brother-in-law Alec Kissock. McCaffertys and Kissocks were friends from County Antrim that worked in Harthill too. Archie and his family were working in the Butte mines and told my grandpa to come out - quick. They were mining for copper, not coal, and there were loads of Irish immigrants, and all kinds of immigrants, working there making good money. It was known as "the richest hill on earth"[26] and Pawn wanted a piece of that for his growing family, and particularly to bring baby Jim over from the Old Country. Butte had been a boomtown for the Irish, Scots, Cornish, Italians and Poles from the late 1800s - early 1900s and in the early 1930s still was one of the best bets to find work for the highest wages in America during the Great Depression.

Andrew McCleary, Pawn's brother.

Detroit, Michigan 1931

CHAPTER 6

BUTTE, MONTANA - 1931

With a loaf of white bread in a brown paper sack, Pawn jumped on a freight train passing through Detroit headed out west for Butte. It took five or six days to travel the 1750 miles to Butte on that train through upper middle America, open, flat country. Butte, named after the high butte that stands beside it, is in Silver Bow County in the Rocky Mountain range that begins in Canada and runs from north to south diagonally through Montana. The town sits on the Rocky Mountains at the Continental Divide. Montana and is beautiful, rough, wild country, green, mountainous and filled up with pine trees. Compared to the desolate Dakotas that the freight train rolled through it was all the more beautiful. When Pawn arrived there was one slice of bread left in that brown paper sack. He was a thin and wiry man to start with and now was severely undernourished. He walked into town and found the Kissock's house where Archie stayed. The strange town of Butte with its taverns, gambling halls, brothels and all manner of debauchery was shocking and very foreign for a reserved Scotsman from small mining village halfway between Edinburgh and Glasgow.

Pawn approached the Kissock's house, which was nicer than most of the shacks in Butte, and rapped on the door. It was late at night and the only light was from the porch-light bulb glowing over his head. The man of the house, Alec Kissock, was sitting in the kitchen looking out the screen door when Pawn knocked. Pawn was thin and hunched over with weariness from the long trip - his tall, skinny body a hook shape, standing sideways in the low light. Mr. Kissock said, "Who in the hell is that buzzard on our porch?" Pawn said, "It's me, Jim McCleary from Scotland." They let him in to sit down and get some food from Delia, his wife. Thereafter his nickname was Buzzard. Archie was ecstatic to see his old friend from home and they set about finding my grandpa some work. The Kissocks let Pawn stay in an extra room, in an outbuilding on Kissock's Hill. Delia McCafferty, Archie's sister was married to Alec Kissock.

All able bodied men and boys, and sometimes women and little children, in Butte worked in the copper mines in the hundreds of miles of tunnels that ran under the town itself. The company in charge was called Anaconda and a company town of the same name was established some 20 miles or so from Butte. Butte had ethic neighborhoods for the Irish, Welsh, Finnish, Cornishmen, Italians, Eastern Europeans, Poles and other ethnic groups.[28] When my grandpa got there in the early 1930s, the jobs available in the mines were controlled by the Italians (my dad Jack's pronunciation: EYE-talians) in town and were hard to break into, especially for a Mick fresh off the boat from Scotland, with a noticeable brogue and emaciated frame.

Since Pawn had already put in ten years in the coal mines in Scotland he was not that enchanted with the idea of mining anyway. He found a job in one of the several slaughterhouses in Butte as an upgrade. It was Hansen's Packing Plant. I can't imagine more unpleasant work than on a slaughterhouse kill floor, but at least it was above ground and wasn't stalking and killing vermin like his father did. This was Pawn's best choice at the time. His job at Hansen's was processing horse meat for K-rations that were needed for the military. Many horses were slaughtered each day and the meat cooked in pressure cookers. Pawn's part was to scoop the hot meat out of the vat and into barrels for cooling and later shipping. Each load on the pitchfork weighed 150 lbs. and it took three scoops to fill each barrel, then they were cooled and capped and sent to the military. Pawn also went up to Canada: north of Edmonton, Alberta and did some "cowboying" (my dad's saying) and repairing fences in what they call the Peace River country for about eight months.

Meanwhile, Grandma Jean and Betty were still living in Detroit and Grandma was working at the Ford Mansion. Betty was taken care of by Pawn's brother Andy and his family. At this juncture, fall and winter 1930 James McCleary's small family was from three different places: Jean from Northern Ireland, James and baby Jim from Scotland, Betty a Canadian, and any future family from America. Baby Jim was living with grandma Rachel McAleese Hunter in Scotland and growing up under the loving care of his grandparents and extended Hunter family of which there were many members in Jean's family of twelve siblings.

One of my aunts said that growing up in America with all the family back in the Old Country was hard and lonely for the McClearys. Back in Harthill and likewise County Antrim there was no shortage of grandparents, siblings, cousins on the McCleary and Hunter sides both. Starting out in Butte there were no grandparents ever or relations for quite some time. My family began to make some lifelong bonds with friends and neighbors that have lasted until this very day and would take the place of some of what they left behind in the Old Country. A few of these families have been like kin to the McClearys for almost 100 years. They are the Kissocks, the Watts, and the Schulers.

My grandpa lived in the Kissocks servant's shack or bunkhouse on their property called Kissocks Hill. This area is now on Utah Avenue in Butte. The Kissocks' spread was a little more high class than most in Butte. Pawn and Archie McCafferty worked and ran around Butte together in those days. Pawn was a slightly built man but "165 pounds of pure fury" when provoked. While out at a bar in Butte with Archie, three guys started giving Buzzard, who was new in town, "some static" and he unleashed the fury and knocked all three guys out right there in the barroom. I guess after that it got around that he was tough and no-one messed with him as much. Pawn would fight if necessary but it was not fueled by alcohol, he was one of the few in the family not a problem drinker. So Pawn was not a "drinker."

The 4 Mile

Pawn saved enough money working at the slaughterhouse to send for Jean and baby Betty. Grandma and the baby left Detroit and they travelled inside a proper train - not in a freight car- to Butte. After a joyous reunion, my grandparents, both 24 years old found a place to live on the 4 Mile in Butte off Harrison Ave, on the street now Paxon. The 4 Mile was a flat and desolate hamlet on the outskirts of Butte and in the distance you could see the Rocky Mountains hugged by trees and capped with snow. It was an unincorporated, rural area four miles from Uptown Butte. It was a poor area, especially in the depression era 1930s. The 4 Mile was home to a mix of Irish, English, Welsh and Italian mining families. Most other parts of Butte were ethnically homogenous: Finntown, Dublin Gulch, Italians in Meaderville, the Cornish in Centerville to name a few neighborhoods. In the book, *The Miners*, they talk about the Cousin Jacks, a slang name for the Welsh miners. When asked if they knew anyone that could mine they always said, "Well I have a Cousin Jack back home in Wales that could surely come and work…" The women from Wales were then called the Cousin Janes too, the Janes were great domestics. Some Italians lived on the stretch of 4 Mile where the McClearys and Watts lived: the Pachecos. Mr. Pacheco was a barber, Mrs. Pacheco was a homemaker and they had twelve kids. The Pacheco boys enjoyed hiding, jumping out and beating the shit out of the older Watts boys for fun.

The McClearys and the Watts lived a few houses apart out at the 4 Mile. Nearby is the Mountain View Cemetery and back then there was a dog racing track for greyhounds. The dog track brought in lots of riff-raff, drunks, and gamblers to the 4 Mile. One drifter that slept at the dog track, named Albert Bochecker, came around the McCleary and Watts houses to "cad" meals. Jean and Margaret didn't have any extra really, but always found food for Mr. Bochecker. Grandma Jean loved the Watts' big German shepherd named Pooch, the one that pulled the Indian travois (like a sled) in the Butte parade. She gave him treats and food scraps. The sweet, big old dog ran back and forth between its two homes.

The eastside of Butte was the tough part of town. Uptown Butte, built on top of a mountain, is hilly with lots of establishments for drinking, enjoying the company of a woman, eating, gambling and whatever else the workers did in their little bit of off time. They say for every bar in Butte there was a brothel to go with it to serve the customers. The library, the hospital and the business offices for the mining companies were uptown. Under it all ran the rats' maze of mines that kept Butte alive. Butte was literally perched atop a spider web of mine shafts with 20 - maybe more – black, looming headframes for each mine mixed in amongst the buildings and houses. In Butte proper there was not much green or grass or trees, just dust and industry. The nicer town of Anaconda, about 26 miles northwest of Butte, was built by "the Company" for the managers and upper echelon of the mining community in town. The further out from Butte you went the prettier and more Montana like it was. My grandparents' first real home in the US was in this industrial town with smelters stacks puking out smoke and immigrants from all over the world trying to make a go of it in America – out west.

Margaret Watts was my very private grandma's best friend for over 40 years (until my grandma died) and the fathers, Earl and Pawn, friends until they died, and the two families close for 80 years. Pawn and Earl had each other's back and when one found a good opportunity, they found a way to pull the other one in. There was a true Watts-McCleary alliance to make life better for both families.

In 1931, my aunt Beverley Jane was born in the house at the 4 Mile. Betty Rachel and Beverley were close in age – only 14 months apart. In 1933, a third sister Anna Mae was born at the 4 Mile house as well. The house was fairly small and rough with a wood stove and an outhouse, so no electricity or indoor plumbing. The second brother, Robert Hunter (called Tony all his life) namesake of Robert Hunter, Jean's dad, was born two years later in 1935. Uncle Tony got the nickname 'Tony' because as a kid he had some sort of illness with a rheumy cough that made him talk funny and someone started calling him Tony because of that. Uncle Tony was a darling little boy with the striking dark hair and brows of his mother, porcelain skin and green eyes. All the rest of the family had and would have blue eyes. My Uncle Howard, now 69, as a kid thought everyone in the world had blue eyes; he didn't know there was any other color. Bright, intense blue eyes are the hallmark of a McCleary.

In this time period at the 4 Mile, Grandma Jean was pregnant again and gave birth to a stillborn child. My grandmother did not have an easy life and was always on her feet working as a waitress even while pregnant. And never complained. In total she would give birth ten times, though she was a frail and petite woman, and eight children would survive into adulthood.

Just one year later in 1936 Donna Lea was born, but in the Catholic hospital in Butte instead of at the house at 4 Mile. Her birth certificate from the hospital says "No Name McCleary" because Jim and Jean didn't name her until sometime after they got her home. Her son had a band, "The No Name McClearys" in Montana many years later. Aunt Donna later changed the spelling of her name to spelling Dona in high school – to be cool she says. She is the only McCleary kid from this family born in a hospital. Even she doesn't know why she was born there and later attended Catholic school when all the others attended public school. I told her that they knew she'd be the spiritual giant that she is today. She is, she's an incredible person.

When Grandma Jean was in labor with Dona in St. James hospital her best pal and sidekick Margaret Watts came to sit with her and wait while Jean popped out kid number six. Margaret was a spirited, funny, no-nonsense woman. Hungry, Margaret had ordered a cheeseburger and brought it into the maternity room with her. Much to her dismay, it had a big slice of strong onion on it. Mrs. Watts opened the dirty linen chute and threw the onion down with the hospital linens. Aunt Dona was born in a room with the faint scent of onions. She was the only McCleary hospital baby but it was homey with the food smell, just like 4 Mile.

The Watts family matched the McClearys kid for kid four times and then Margaret officially dropped out of the birthing race with Jean. The Watts kids are Shirley, born 1933, and best friend of my Aunts Betty and Bev; Robert born 1934; Jim born 1936, and David born 1938, all the boys were close pals of my dad Jack and my uncles Tony and Howard. Margaret and Jean were midwives for each other on the 4 Mile and only one kid each was born in St. James hospital uptown. Both Jimmy Watts and Dona were winter babies and, at least in Jim's case, he was born in the hospital because the temperature on his birthday was 61 degrees below zero, coldest day in Montana history and they couldn't keep him alive if he was born at home. His dad, Earl had to light a fire, literally, under the car to thaw the oil to get Margaret to St. James Hospital in Uptown Butte to deliver the baby Jim.

For seven years Pawn continued to work at the slaughterhouse Hansen Packing and then finally relented and got on at the copper mine to keep the family going. Descending into the mine was the last thing he wanted to do, but that was how you made money in Butte. Pawn signed on with the United Mine Workers labor union and went to work mining again. It was some of the best money to be made in America at the time. But the work was dangerous as hell and really physically hard, he was a mucker.

No one in the pit wants to be a mucker, it was that difficult. The blast monkeys, what they called the dynamite guys, would blast on a vein and the muckers would muck out the ore, dust and debris. At that point men with carpentry skills, which Pawn and Earl acquired, would jump in and build a stope, which was kind of a wooden brace and a ladder and then a platform. The blast monkeys would blast again. The mucker would open a trap door in the platform and all the ore and debris would fall on his head and he'd get up in there and muck it off the platform. In time Pawn and Earl got really good at the wood working part of this job in the pit. Everyone working in the mine was in the Miner's Union and the old miners played lots of pranks on the greenhorns. Before a new guy could go in the mine, he had to sign the union card shoved in his face by one of the old timers that growled, "*Sign it now!*"

Venus Alley

Grandma Jean waitressed at a restaurant over on Harrison Ave for the lady who also owned and madamed the Dumas Brothel. The owner/Madame was Ann Cody; I am told she was the sister of Buffalo Bill Cody. Let me be clear, Grandma Jean only worked in Ann Cody's restaurant –not the whore house! My Aunt Dona, who goes with my uncle to Butte every St. Patrick's Day for the celebration in the streets (known as the wildest party in the west), recently misspoke on the Dumas Brothel tour and said her mom worked for Ann Cody, the Madame but forgot to say it was in the restaurant. I am right here setting the record straight. Waitress! The Dumas brothel was the longest running brothel in the US, shockingly not closing for business till 1982 when the final Madame got arrested and jailed for tax evasion. The authorities in Butte, between 1880 and 1940, turned a blind eye to the prostitution trade because it brought so much money into downtown Butte, to both the brothels and the pimps, and the legitimate businesses like noodle shops, saloons, dress shops and boarding houses for the women to live. The pimps in Butte were called "secretaries" to try and class up their job description.

Women from all over the world worked in the cribs on Venus Alley, which in earlier days was called Pleasant Alley, near Mercury and Galena Streets. The little cubicles, or cribs, where the women showed off their wares at a front window and conducted their business were about twelve feet wide but had a corner sink, a small bathroom and closet. The more high class women worked out of parlor houses, which Dumas was one, and were generally white women. The parlor houses like the Windsor, the Victoria, the Irish World and the Dumas had huge plate glass front windows where the "escorts" could be looked over before the man even came through the door. The ladies on The Line or Venus Alley and the brothels connected to it were called Jew Jess, Mexican Maria and so on based on their nationality or religion.[29] Some of the brothels had 100 or more girls working out of them. They served the miners getting off shift, most of Butte was single men, and so the girls worked in shifts too. In the crib there was a callbox for the girl to order food or alcohol from the near businesses or call for help if she needed it.

In the early days 1880 or so, the prostitution trade in Butte was wide open and obvious. The parlor house girls shopped in the fancy dress and hat shops on the main street and guys squired them around openly. In later times the flesh trade was shoved underground, literally, and the brothel owners built cribs underground for the women to work out of so men could pass in and out secretly. Under Venus Alley was a labyrinth of tunnels and little rooms with no water and a chamber pot.[30] In 1940 or so both ends of Venus Alley were boarded off and signs said no one under 21 could enter were posted, although many miners were well under that age, starting work at twelve or fourteen. Man enough to work, not man enough to come to Venus Alley or The Tenderloin it was called. The women from the brothels were not allowed to be seen on the street until 5 pm each night.

After Venus Alley was fenced in, the brothel owners then built the rows of cribs inside two or three stories high as well as those underground. The prostitutes in their individual windows, scantily dressed even in cold winter rapped on the glass at passing men with thimbles, rings, chopsticks, anything to attract the attention of a potential customer. They say it sounded like a telegraph office along The Line with all the tapping.

During Prohibition in the 1920s, evangelists flocked to Butte to rail against all the sinning going on. The Reverend William Biederwolf said about Butte in 1905: "There is enough legitimate vice to damn the souls of every young man and woman in it," and "Butte, the lowest sinkhole of the West." It was a modern Sodom and Gomorrah some would say. Or "The richest hill on earth," others would say that needed the money to survive.

By 1936, Pawn and Jean saved enough money to send for Jim to come from Harthill, Scotland to Butte, Montana. They were so excited and relieved to finally bring their oldest son to America. They wrote to Jean's mother and got word back that Jim who was six years old didn't want to come, would not come. He was accustomed to living with his grandma Rachel Hunter and didn't want to sail across the ocean to live in America with what to him were strangers. He didn't come. Grandma Jean's heart broke again as it had when she sailed on the Andania and left him behind at two months of age. Even though Grandma had given birth to five or six more babies in the meantime, she still felt the loss and wanted her oldest son with her. It was not going how she had planned.

My grandpa was a moonshiner on the side to make extra money, at this time there were six kids to support, including Jim in Scotland. The Kissocks operated stills and had a going concern for moonshining back on Kissocks Hill. Pawn was part of the operation and they brewed some potent liquor to sell and bring in extra dough. There never seemed to be enough, money that is. A Mick friend from Butte always said that the 4 Mile area should be named Hellsport, because life was so hard out there and everyone was so poor. The Irish in New York City had the Hell's Kitchen, Irish in Chicago in prohibition days had Little Hell. It seems fitting that Butte should have had its own hellish Irish section too: Hellsport.

In that humble house on 4 Mile, Jean gave birth to another baby girl in November 1938 – Sharon McCleary. Little Sharon was born with a hole in her back, which was spina bifida, and contracted pneumonia not long after birth. She only lived for one month and died at St. James Hospital on December 21st, right before Christmas in 1938.[31] My Aunt Betty who was 8 at the time remembered how sad everyone was especially Grandma Jean. She was devastated to lose her baby and that Christmas was horrible for the McClearys. Betty helped get little Sharon ready for her wake at the funeral home. They dressed her in a tiny dress with velvet shoes and Grandma Jean tucked a blanket in around Sharon in the little white casket.

The last rites, as they called it in the Montana Standard newspaper were in the Paradise Room of the Duggan & Merrill Mortuary and her final resting place is in the Mountain View Cemetery in Butte. The James McClearys were not Catholics but the wake and the last rites must have been the way they did all funerals in Butte. She was buried under an austere cement marker that read "Baby McCleary" because they were so poor. In the mid-1990s, my dad, Jack, Aunt Betty, and Aunt Bev went to Butte and replaced little Sharon's marker with a proper gravestone that now marks the grave.

Most important to me and my story: Jack Alexander was born next at the house on 4 Mile on February 10, 1940. Or as my dad always said, "two-ten-forty." My dad was named Jack. Not John with Jack for a nickname, but just Jack. Pawn and Grandma Jean named my dad after Jack Kissock, one of the Old Country friends. The Alexander part was named after Alexander McAleese, born 1815 in Antrim. My dad loved the middle name Alexander and was proud to be named after his Irish ancestor. Betty was the eldest kid in the home at age 12 and was very aware of Jack's impending arrival. She, along with everyone else, was deeply affected by the death of baby Sharon and was hoping the birth of the next baby would go well. Margaret Watts, Jean's part-time midwife was there for the birth.

Betty was sent outside while Jack was born but peered through the window with curiosity. Inside she saw the bustle of a baby coming and was shocked to see blood. A young girl, she didn't know birth involved so much blood - bloody sheets, blood tinged water. Shocked, she wished she hadn't looked through the window. Later she got to meet her third brother, Jack Alexander. He was in perfect shape, no problems with the back like baby Sharon had been born with on hers. Grandma Jean and Pawn were so relieved and pleased with the new baby. The kids aged 12, 10, 9, 7, 5, and 4 where happy with the latest McCleary too. Jack was a husky baby, had the squareish face of Grandma Jean, the mandatory bright blue eyes and fair skin. I have a photo of dad as an infant in a gown sitting up in a rocking chair out in the dirt yard. Grass didn't grow very well in Butte, at the 4 Mile.

Grandma Jean's younger sister Elizabeth (Lizzie) Hunter Hartman came to live in Butte around this time with her husband and small daughter. Jean was the eldest child of twelve and Lizzie the next child after Jean. They were very close and when she arrived, having come to America through Canada a few years before, she and her family moved in with my grandparents, and all the kids, at the 4 Mile. My grandma was delighted to have her sister in America at all and especially living in Butte. Aunt Lizzie, Howard Hartman and their children eventually rented the house next door on Paxon and moved out. I am sure Pawn was relieved; eleven people in the house tested his patience.

In old black and white photos, the McCleary and Watts kids and their mothers, Jean and Margaret, are dressed up in cowboy and patriotic gear for a 4th of July parade in Uptown Butte. The caption that Mrs. Watts wrote on the photo under says "some pumpkins." Which must have meant: look how cute and funny we were. Everyone is smiling, having fun and all the kids are adorable in their makeshift costumes posing on the cobblestone street amongst the uptown storefronts in Butte, around 1939 or so. The kids wore hats with dingle balls attached to the brim and cowboy vests and boots with miscellaneous scarves tied jauntily on their necks. Where they got money for costumes is a mystery to me since they were all poor as hell. Little Shirley Watts, who was the oldest of all the kids, won the first prize in the parade that day by leading her dog Pooch, a German Shepard, pulling a doll in an Indian travois that her dad Earl had made for the occasion.

Butte was a town that really loved parades, still does actually, the St. Patrick's Day parade and festivities in Butte are a notorious drunkfest in the west. In old-time Butte they had the Miner's Day parade, 4th of July parade, St. Patrick's Day parade and the Doll Parade, among others. According to the Montana Standard on April 6, 1941, little Anna Mae McCleary strolled an antique Scottish doll stroller in the doll parade through Butte and stole the show taking first prize that year. I wonder though, how in the hell did this 100 year old stroller, as it was reported, get to Butte from Scotland, did someone bring it on the boat? The Miner's Day parade was a big deal and all the miners would march through Butte under their union banner and go all the way to Columbia Gardens for physical competitions of the miners' skills.[32]

Columbia Gardens

The magnificent Columbia Gardens were a beloved Butte landmark built by one of the copper kings, William Clark, and later purchased by the Anaconda Company. The amusement park opened amid great fanfare in

1899 and stayed open until it burned down (very suspiciously) in the 1970s. Columbia Gardens was Disneyland-type, magical place built for the workers in the mines and their families. Unlike industrial Butte with torn up streets, steel headframes in amongst the shacks that were houses and powder dust, Columbia Gardens was a huge, green 68 acre park with manicured flower gardens and rides and other amusements for the kids and adults alike. It was an oasis, magic for the poor and rich of Butte, especially the children.

On the hillside of the park there were big logos in flowers of a harp, a nod to the Irish in Butte, and a huge butterfly and the ever-present Anaconda logo. The people of Butte had a love/hate relationship with the Anaconda Company, but the Gardens were definitely in the love column. The mine was named after the anaconda snake by one of the early prospectors and the mining company adopted the name later. Anaconda really was like a powerful snake in the lives of the miners and their families over the years. Some of the political cartoons of the time show the huge, muscular snake, the anaconda, weaving through the town, the workers and their lives.

Columbia Gardens was free to the public and once inside each ride cost 15 cents. It had the only roller coaster (the townspeople called it "rollycoaster") in the state of Montana. It was a rickety wooden affair with three frightening looking levels. The car somehow stayed on the wooden rails, single cars as opposed to a train of cars. There was a beautiful carousel with handmade horses that were repainted in every off season. There was a zoo with mostly native Montana animals: bear, moose, coyote, elk and so on. The Company ran an electric trolley from Uptown Butte to the Columbia Gardens east of town and in later years a bus operated on the route. It was a 20 minute ride either inside the trolley or, more fun than that, hanging off the side of the trolley that passed through tough East Butte on its way out of town. The 4 Mile is beyond that in the rural outskirts of town.

One day of the week was Kid's Day – Thursday - and the rides were cheaper for kids and the trolley or bus was free. Many of the operators would take pity on the poor urchins and let them go for free on Kid's Day. It was a wonderland for the young and old of Butte. The large pavilion that looked like a castle at Columbia Gardens was used for dances and proms, and was a venue for some of the Big Bands of the 1940s. The pavilion dance floor held 700-1000 dancers, and was full at some of the events in its heyday.

In some family photos, Grandma Jean and Margaret Watts are at the Gardens with their arms full of babies and more kids around their feet. The children are wearing bonnets and sitting on the grass and the fence around their mothers. In one picture, it was a sunny day and Jean and Margaret, also wearing sun hats, brought a picnic lunch for the children. Columbia Gardens had acres of trees, grass (which was nonexistent in Butte), streams, hiking trails and the like. When the kids were a little older, they could ride the bus out and go on their own. And by a little older, I mean they could walk on their own. Many Butte mothers shipped their kids off to the Gardens on their own to have fun. The gardens had an enclosed garden full of violets where kids could pick a bouquet of violets or pansies to take home to their mother.

Not so idyllic was the trip to the park when Anna Mae McCleary lost her shoes in the creek. Anna lost one shoe in the creek at the Gardens and found Beverley, her big sister, and told her what happened. In a flash of brilliance Bev said, "I know how to find your shoe. We'll put the other shoe in the creek where you lost the first one and where it floats to and stays is where we'll find the first shoe." Anna thought this sounded perfectly logical. After testing the theory, Anna Mae went home with two lost shoes. My uncle said she was inconsolable on the bus back because losing your shoes was a major offense in those poor days.

Little Jimmy Watts also had a rough trip to the gardens when he was about five or six. He rode the bus out with all the Watts and McCleary kids (probably about 10 of them) and sometime during the day Jim tried to jump the stream that ran through the gardens and fell in and got his pants all brown and stained up to the crotch. The smelters in Butte that spit out all the smoke also dumped their liquid waste into all the waterways in and around Butte. This residue on Jim was from the smelters but looked suspiciously brown and poop-like. He was a smart boy and knew if he got on the bus back to Butte (and their mothers weren't with them) all the kids would tease him mercilessly and he would be shamed forever. When his big sister Shirley told him to get on the bus with the rest of the kids, Jimmy did. But he just walked onto the shuttle bus back to Butte in the front door, walked down the aisle and off the bus by the back door. Sister Shirley didn't have a clue.

Then he walked home. Columbia Gardens was about 20 miles outside of Butte and Jim was a little boy with short legs. It was a hell of a long dark walk. Finally Jim stumbled onto the cemetery which he kind of knew was near the house on 4 Mile. It was 8 pm and pitch dark and as he got near the house he could see police cars, policemen and civilians on foot, men on horses, all searching for him in the dark. There were flashing lights from the cop cars and people in full panic mode searching for the little boy that had been lost since early in the day. So he trudged in with his stained pants and everyone was overjoyed and relieved to see him. All his family, especially his mother Margaret hugged and kissed him and welcomed him home. The McClearys were happy, the Butte cops and county sheriff were happy. It was pure joy. After the wonderful reunion everyone left and Jim got his butt swatted with a strap by his short mother, who was the disciplinarian in the Watts family, and told to never venture off alone again.

Generations of Butte natives remember Columbia Gardens fondly and wistfully with its smell of buttered popcorn (real melted butter poured over) in greasy brown paper bags from the popcorn lady Mrs. Kelly. They remember the music of the calliope, the family BBQs and birthday parties, the big man-made lake with the steep chutes you could ride down into it, and the hiking paths in the woods. On the film, Remembering Columbia Gardens, one of the men that grew up with it, said "it was a complete departure from everyday life." It was a paradise, especially to the poor kids of Butte. The McCleary squad of a half dozen was certainly in that category. The elder McCleary sisters, Betty and Bev and Shirley Watts attended dances and school functions at the Gardens. It was a spectacular place to see bands like Tommy Dorsey or attend a school prom. Every important social event in Butte was held at the Gardens ballroom or grounds.

In the 1970s, Columbia Gardens caught on fire under strange circumstances when the mining company was blasting the Berkeley Pit. The Pit wiped out many neighborhoods of old Butte for open pit mining to access the copper left under the town. The Pit had surrounded the gardens and after the fire from "so called" faulty wiring the grounds were blasted away too. The only thing remaining from Columbia Garden is the old water tower. In the documentary, Remembering Columbia Gardens, many old timers get choked up and some cry when they relive the loss of Columbia Gardens that was part of Butte life from 1899 to 1974. It was a special place for generations of Butte citizens, their own private heaven in the middle of Montana, so unexpected and so unlike the rough life in Butte the hard core mining town.

Once when little Jackie was a toddler at the 4 Mile he was playing with his mother's lipstick case. Grandma Jean always wore bold lipstick, fashionable glasses and earrings to work with her uniform, even though she was a waitress she always looked good. This day Jack stuck the lipstick cover, the cylinder in his mouth and accidentally sucked it in. His older sisters Bev and Betty were right there and saw it happen. Jack couldn't breathe and started to turn blue. The girls screamed for help and luckily Pawn was there. He calmly took Jack, opened his little mouth and with long slender fingers was able to extract that case from his throat.

Around this time, when the McCleary family had seven kids in Butte, group photos taken professionally start to show up. I call the kids in these photos the McCleary 7, kind of like the Magnificent 7. It surprises me that they found the money for portraits and that they were so well dressed and shined up in these photos. Aunt Bev said that they were poor but were always clean and well dressed. In the first of these black and white photos taken in Butte my dad is a babe in arms - his oldest sister Betty's arms. The next formal family photo is when Howard is a baby, so three years later, and also being held eldest sister Betty (nickname Bumps). A couple of years later, there are more of Jack and Howard together in sailor suits. The kids are shined up with bows in the girls' hair and pomade slicking over the hair of the little boys.

It must have been important to my grandma and grandpa, probably just to Jean, to have portraits of their children captured in time. I am grateful to have them now to see the faces of my people and how they resemble my own children, especially Bella, and nieces and nephews and even me. They say I look like Aunt Beverley, and I guess that I do. Strangers in Richland, like the post office clerk, ask if I am Bev's daughter. Just out of the blue. These family portraits continued all the way until my dad was a teen and the elder McCleary kids were ready to leave home. The men in the McCleary photos always pose in a line with arms akimbo; I think it's genetic. About five years ago I told my dad that I was going to submit the cutest picture of the McCleary 7 from Butte to the magazine, "Irish America."[33] On the back page they feature family pictures that represent Irish immigrants in America doing Irish immigrant stuff. My dad was always thinking, and he said, "Jeezus Sis, don't say too much in that caption below the picture. Someone is likely to read that and come out west and shake us down."

Aunt Betty said that their dad would warm up the kids' shoes and socks in the wood stove before they trekked off to school from the house at the 4 Mile. The two eldest went to the Hawthorne School, except for Aunt Dona who went to the one year of Catholic school and was taught by the nuns. The younger kids attended Emerson School and that's where the Watts boys went too. I have a picture of Aunt Betty and Aunt Beverley posing in a class photo on the Hawthorne School steps looking beautiful in their floor length gowns, for their junior high graduation in the 8th grade.

The two eldest sisters were in the same grade; Bev started school at 5 and Betty 6. Aunt Bev has the McCleary look in the picture and looks very much like me and my niece – or I guess we look like her. Genetics are a powerful thing. In the 1990s my aunts, Bev and Betty, along with my dad Jack went back to the Hawthorne School in Butte and the girls had their picture taken there on those steps again. This was the trip where they got their baby sister Sharon a real headstone in the Mountain View Cemetery and they discovered an article about my dad from the 1944 Butte newspaper.

Aunt Beverley, now 80 and as striking as ever, like she drank from the fountain of youth –blue eyes, fair skin, auburn hair - said that the Hawthorne School was on the west side of town over by the golf course in Butte and all the rich kids went there. Bev and Betty walked from the 4 Mile to the school which was quite a distance and were among the few poor kids that went to school there. Aunt Bev said she never thought about her and Betty and the rest of the McCleary kids being poor; that she noticed the other kids had nicer clothes, but didn't care about that. She did notice that the food they brought to school to eat looked really delicious and wished for some of that rich kid food.

Aunt Betty, her older sister, was shy and Bev always had to stick up for her with the kids, even fist fight with the kids to defend Betty. In Butte the kids were tough, really tough and if you wanted a moment's peace you had to stand up for yourself. There was a lot of rivalry and fighting between schools in Butte and the kids had a rumble going all the time for some reason or another. You had to be tough to make it in Butte. Butte was a badass mining camp and is still known as a rough western town. If you grew up in Butte and survived, it's a badge of honor.

Mining Town Life

Speaking of fights, back in Butte in the 1940s, the town was rough, wild and dangerous but one of the best places in the US to make money. Bar fights were as commonplace as having a drink or taking a piss. The work in the pits was hellish and very hard – mentally and physically. The miners were, literally, a mile deep under the town with dynamite blasting off all around them. Pawn had already put in ten years in the coal mines of Scotland, childhood years, so the copper mines of Butte, while familiar must have been terrible for my grandpa. Although he always said that work in the US was so easy, compared to work in the mines in Scotland, that it was a joke to him. He thought American workers had it easy.

He and Earl built wood and cement frames to build the stopes for the hard rock mining – copper was hard rock mining. Hard rock mining is defined as ore that could be removed only by blasting, as opposed to ore that could be worked out with hand tools. The coal mining in Scotland had been drift mining. The stopes formed a framework for the tunnel and shored up the work area. This is where Jim and Earl got their first shot at carpentry work and realized that maybe it was their ticket out of mining and especially a ticket out for their boys. Neither wanted their sons to work in the mines of Butte or anywhere else. Pawn told himself when he came from Scotland that no son of his would ever work a mine in America.

Butte was a union town and if you worked in the mine you were generally in the Miner's Union. There was trouble in the town between the Union and the mine owners over better pay and conditions and then local politicians got involved to further complicate the volatile situation. There were strikes, buildings burned, marches and people hurt and killed in the melee around these emotional issues for years. The reality of the Labor Union vs. the mine owners' conflict was made clear to Jim Watts, and his older brother, when he was about six years old. Their dad Earl said, "Boys, get in the car, we are going uptown." Driving from 4 Mile to the busy town center, ahead on a light post on a corner there was something odd. As they got closer, Jim was horrified and stunned to see that it was a black man hanged by the neck from the light post. Earl said, "That, boys, is a scab, he crossed the picket line to work in the mine. Don't ever be a scab. That's what happens."

We have family friends, also from Butte that recall the Irish miners walking down from the mine at night and into town after their ten or twelve hour shifts, which ran around the clock. While walking in a group with their headlamps on, the miners sang Irish songs, Irish ditties our friends call them. It was an eerie sight, the miners coming down in an illuminated, singing mass from the pit in the dark. The smelter in Butte, used to process the copper, was called "the Man Killer" it caused so many deaths from its toxic fallout. The flakes from the stack, which was the tallest stack in Montana, fell like snow on the town. When the housewives and boarding house owners did their laundry, they had to shake the ash from the Man Killer off of the linens before bringing them inside. The grandpa in the Mitchell family died young after the toxins from the smelter destroyed his nose cartilage. The man killer was just that, and it killed plenty of young men by attacking their respiratory system too. Our friends in Butte lived in the house that was the home of the mistress of Marcus Daly, one of the two Copper Kings. Many families living presently in Washington State have ties to Butte and the copper mining there.

Pawn brought home all the money he could and Grandma Jean waitressed at the Cody restaurant on Harrison Ave. to do the same. They were poor but the children were busy and involved in activities and events in Butte. In the Montana Standard newspaper, there are little articles and blurbs documenting the McCleary kids' movements. Aunts Betty and Beverley and Shirley Watts were in a few clubs, like Camp Fire Girls. The older sisters played on the Y-basketball team. Jackie McCleary, attended a first birthday party for a rich little boy, Ward Thompson III, on Harrison Ave. along with Grandma Jean. He was only one himself. I'm sure Jean knew the rich family through her waitressing work at the Cody restaurant. Grandma Jean and Aunt Betty at 11 were in an auto accident riding with another family. So the McClearys made the Butte society pages as it were. Also in the Montana Standard on September 29, 1940 my grandfather became a US citizen along with a handful of other Butte residents of various nationalities. He had been in the US for 10 years at that time. "18 Citizenship Papers Granted" was the headline. My grandmother and Aunt Betty became citizens later. They were finally Americans. Not Irish, not Scottish, not Canadians, but Americans – Citizens of the United States of America.

No one had much at the 4 Mile so the Watts boys, Robbie and Jimmy and my uncle Tony, because Jack and Howard were too little, had to make some dough of their own. The boys sold newspapers to the miners in the taverns and they would invite them in for a drink even though they were just eight or ten. So the boys were hanging around the bars quite a bit. At that time in 1940s Butte there was a bottle cap refund program. So the little boys hung around the back of the bar and when they had an opening one of them scaled the fence with a gunny sack while the others stood watch. In the enclosure behind the bar was a barrel full of bottle caps that people had returned for the refund at the bar. The boy inside the fence filled the gunny sack as quick as he could and threw it, hefted it, somehow got it over the fence to his accomplices. Then they would drag it around front and take inside to the barman to get the refund.

The boys ran this scam at the bars in Butte and the Coca Cola Bottling Company. Same operation at Coca Cola: over the fence, fill the bag, heft it over, drag it around, coolly hand over to the Coca Cola guy, pocket the money, head back to 4 Mile. Sometimes they stopped by the candy shop for a little reward from the spoils of their grifting. The barmen and the soft drink merchant must have known what was happening and just gave them the money out of charity. And as a reward for their balls and pluck.

In black and white photos of the McCleary and Watts kids, they are in raggedy overalls, some with one strap hanging down and some too short, and other miscellaneous garb while sitting on old cars in dusty fields. Sometimes the girls were out in the snow in dresses with bare legs. There was an old Ford at the 4 Mile that was a prop for a lot of photos of the kids. Some of the houses at 4 Mile were covered with black tar-paper on the outside, waiting for some siding that never arrived. It was the 1940s and times were tough but the two families had a damn good time. The McClearys were big singers - everyone sang. Aunt Dona said she learned to love singing from her father and to this day she will belt out "Mrs. Murphy's Chowder" at any time. Aunt Bev also said that Pawn sang all the time and she remembers that most about her dad.

The houses that Pawn and Earl Watts built on the 4 Mile were small with odd flat roofs. Neither of them knew how to make a pitched roof. Since the 4 Mile was an unincorporated part of Butte, there were no building codes to work to and they could get away with it. Hilarious, because they would both be big operators in the Carpenters Union in the coming years. There was no indoor plumbing and in the Montana winter going to the toilet was a bitter, cold affair at -30 F. Jimmy Watts remembers walking through tunnels in the snow to get around during a storm. The city of Butte also brought out equipment to push the snow into berms on vacant lots, then the firemen came with the water truck and filled the big square with water. Ice skating rinks!

In later years at the 4 Mile the fathers, Jim and Earl, dug long, long trenches to bring plumbing in their houses. Up until that time all the McCleary kids bathed in a big metal tub that had two compartments and was about 18 inches deep. Bath day was Sunday. The water was heated on the wood stove and the littlest ones bathed first, two at a time, on up the ranks to Betty and Bev the oldest. Over the years Jim and Earl made improvements and tacked on additions to the houses but they always had the signature flat roof. Those handmade houses still stand in Butte today – modest houses on Paxon near Harrison Ave. and the Mountain View Cemetery.

Carpenters

My grandpa finally decided to join the Carpenters Union in Butte and officially learn a new trade to carry him through to retirement and get out of the mining business once and for all. Skilled with his hands, down in the mines he had built his share of wood braces and structures. My grandpa and Earl Watts learned how to be carpenters on their own out of an instruction book. After studying and practicing they went to take the carpenters test, which was to build a rustic, large wooden toolbox. Both passed and became Union carpenters. This was the first step away from the mines for my grandpa and a step toward a new life for the McClearys. Those old tool boxes from the life-changing tests are still around in the Watts and McCleary houses here in Washington. Since Butte was such a big Union town and there was a union for everything, Pawn joined the Carpenter rolls without further ado. This affiliation was another step in his lifetime love affair with the Union and all it represented for the working man. Pawn was passionate about the Union. People say that my grandpa was a heavy union man all through his life.

In 1941, World War II was underway in Europe and Earl Watts got a tip on carpenter work in Richland, Washington, in the desert on the eastern side of the state. The government was building a big plant, a secret project, there for the war effort. Work was available for all the trades and the contractors were just ramping up and fast. The Watts family packed up in a two ton truck, sold their flat roof house for $2000 leaving Butte, Montana for Washington State. Earl and Margaret wondered if they would ever see so much money at one time again in their lives.

The baby of the McCleary family was born at the 4 Mile house in 1943: Howard Dale. Grandma Jean gave birth ten times in fifteen years beginning with Uncle Jim in Scotland in 1928 and ending with Uncle Howard ("Howie") in 1943. When Howie was born Grandma Jean was 38. She worked from age fourteen, like my Grandpa, and both always worked hard without complaint to provide for their large family. In 1944, Pawn was 40 and had eight living kids, his dear wife, and had been mining for the better part of 26 years.

Aunt Betty told me that at wartime in the US there was a freeze on travel across the Atlantic and that Jim couldn't have come over in those years because of it. So there was another delay in sending for Jim. Since the war was on, the workers in Butte were mining all the copper they could for the war effort. Grandma Jean and Pawn had their whole gaggle of kids, and Jean's sister Lizzie was living next door with her family out on the 4 Mile. While Pawn worked in the mine and Jean worked in the Cody restaurant, Aunt Betty was in charge of the kids.

St. James Hospital

When Jack was four he got into an accident. Jackie and Howard, age one, and neighborhood kids were playing out in the fields around 4 Mile. There were some cement pipes, big ones, and the kids were horsing around and climbing on them. Jack fell off and into a cement pipe and broke his leg severely. The break was a spiral fracture and very serious. He was scooped up and taken to St. James Hospital in Uptown Butte. The doctors at St. James set his leg in a cast and then set the other in a cast too – for good measure. They must have had a reason, but a lively 4 year old in two full casts from toe to hip was a prison sentence. Then they hoisted both legs up in traction at nearly a 90 degree angle and he stayed that way for four months. He was the only one on the children's ward and the whole floor except for one little girl that was there a short time. She died and was taken away.

There were nurses caring for him but at night he was alone in the hospital bed in the vast room full of empty beds with large windows all around. He cried himself to sleep every night for four months. Some of the nights there was thunder and lightning in the Rocky Mountains around Butte and he was terrified. Dad wished someone would come for him, send for him and take him home to the house at 4 Mile – he'd never been away from home before. To keep him company one of the nurses set up a radio for four year old Jackie to listen to and pass the time. Patriotic songs played to support the boys overseas and keep morale up stateside and Jack listened, sang along and learned all the songs from Butte Radio. When he got out of the hospital after the 120 days in traction, he could croon the wartime tunes like a little Bing Crosby and performed for the public in Butte.

Dad's imprisonment in St. James Hospital was broken up by a few visits from his parents, but they were busy with the other kids and both working so these visits were few. His brothers and sisters, except baby Howard would come around but were not allowed in the hospital – no kids could come in. So the resourceful Little 'Clearys found a way to see Jackie. The hospital was set into a hill and they could gather under Jack's window on the kids' ward. He was at a second floor window so the taller ones would hold the little ones like Tony on their shoulders and they would wave in to their little brother. Jack was a little guy in a white gown with two huge white cigar legs strung up in front of him. He would smile and wave, my dad had a great smile, and seeing his brothers and sisters' heads bob in front of the window once in a while got him through.

61

The hospital was quite far from the house at the 4 Mile so the kids must have come after school to see Jackie. I can't be sure if the traction treatment had anything to do with it, but my dad was really small in stature as a kid and a teen. He always said that he never really grew until he was a sophomore in high school and then shot up to 5'8". But in the years before he was slightly built and very little, Uncle Howard said he was the littlest guy in school except for one other fella.

The Montana Standard newspaper in April 1944 ran a story to highlight the training of the nurses that had been dispatched to World War II and were preparing to go. "Answering Her Country's Call for Service" was the headline and featured a nurse who was caring for my dad. In the old photo, they call him "the cheerful young patient Jackie McCleary…" I went to Butte last year and stopped to see St. James Hospital and imagined my dad there. It is empty and for sale, a hulking shell of a place built into a hilly street in Uptown Butte. This is where my dear Aunt Dona was born and my daddy was suspended by the legs for the four months in 44.

Living in Butte was not easy for anyone –the miners, the prostitutes, the housewives- except maybe for the Anaconda brass. In the Montana Standard newspaper, my grandpa James McCleary appeared in the Aid to the Poor Register on January 19, 1938, which was right after baby Sharon died. He received $26, and it must have bought some food or something the family vitally needed then. In the register, there were many families that received less than $20. I am surprised to see that my grandpa accepted charity because that is very unlike him. It had to have been a desperate situation that sad winter. One of my aunts told me they could charge groceries in Butte at the company store and that when the McClearys finally had to leave Butte that they ran out on a sizable bill in the store. This is hard for me to believe since my grandfather was so honest, and so proud, and self-sufficient. If they really left on the lam from the merchants in Butte it had to be another dire situation. A last resort to keep the "little 'Clearys" (yes, another nickname) alive.

The Watts family, with their four kids and Pooch, bought a small piece of land in Kennewick, the town over from Richland where the Hanford site is located and Earl was working on the site for the Carpenters Union. In the beginning, the Watts lived in the apple picking shed in the orchard on their property then Earl built a small house. So Earl, Margaret and their four kids were the advance party to Washington State. When the Watts got there one of their sons, Robbie, burned his legs in an accident and was seriously injured. This was around the same time Jack broke his leg in

Butte, so Margaret and Jean wrote to each other often to discuss their struggles with their hurt sons, one laid up in Montana, one in Washington. Earl Watts wrote to Pawn and told him work was busting loose in Washington and there were lots of carpenter jobs. Mr. Watts had connections in the Carpenters Union at Hanford and his foreman assured Pawn a job if he came out to the Pacific Northwest.

Above, left to right: Betty McCleary, Shirley Watts, Bev McCleary - 4 Mile, 1935. Below: Jack McCleary w/ Pacheco's house behind, 4 Mile, Butte 1940

Jean McCleary, @ Columbia Gardens w/ Shirley
Watts, Robbie Watts, Bev, Betty and Anna 1933

Above 1940: left to right, Dona, Tony, Betty, Jack-infant, Bev, Anna.
Below 1943: left to right, *Back*, Betty, Howard-infant, Bev. *Middle*,
Anna, Tony, Dona. *Front*, Jack. Butte, Montana

Uptown Butte 4th of July parade, Jean (l) & Margaret
Watts(r) above. Watts and McCleary kids below, 1938

CHAPTER 7

KENNEWICK, WASHINGTON - 1944

Camp Hanford or The Manhattan Project in 1944 was the biggest construction project in the US and had exploded out of a little homesteading area called White Bluffs, on the formidable Columbia River, to an enormous boomtown established to convert uranium to plutonium for the atomic bomb. Camp Hanford was a "Classified Top Secret" project and the vast majority of the workers, other than the very top echelon of managers, scientists and engineers, had no idea what they were building on 550 acres of desert alongside the massive Columbia River in eastern Washington State. All the "hired hands" (my dad Jack's saying) were told that it was for national security and for the war effort - that was all they knew. Eventually there were nine nuclear reactors and ancillary buildings for weapons grade plutonium extraction and finishing and other processes built here. Plutonium from the Hanford site went in one of the bombs - Fat Man - that was dropped on Nagasaki, Japan at the end of the Second World War. At its peak the Hanford project employed 50,000 workers.[34]

I am saddened and uneasy to report that my both grandfathers worked in the plant that made part of one of the bombs that killed so many in Japan at the close of World War II. Any loss of life in war, especially civilians, is tragic. On the other hand, I can understand the Americans' fear of the Germans at that time and the helpful spirit and hard work of all the citizens that flocked to Hanford to make their fortune, yes, but to keep the United States safe too. No-one knew if the Germans would come to America's shores and I am sure that no-one wanted to find out based on what was happening to Europe. From what I know about the climate on the Manhattan Project/Hanford site at that time, no-one was allowed to even ask or question what they were doing. You just did your work. Period.

And at least for the James McCleary family and what they'd been through with the shed-living and driving from state to state you were damned glad to have a job and a way to feed your family. So you just shut up and kept your head down and worked.

Patriotism ran high on the Hanford site and so did wages for all the crafts - welders, carpenters, masons, machinists, millwrights, etc. Some of the world's greatest minds in physics and engineering came to Hanford to build the plant to extract plutonium from uranium. Less than one percent of the Hanford workforce knew that they were making weapons grade plutonium for atomic bombs. It was the best work in the country and Richland was established for the workers at Hanford and their families. It was the fastest built and largest construction project in the United States along with the Hoover Dam. What was once barren desert and sagebrush quickly became a community with a common purpose, though that purpose was pretty vague.

In some of the cartoons published in the Hanford worker newsletters at the time there is one that speaks to the level of awareness of the workers. It's a cartoon of a little boy talking to other little boys in a cartoon Richland saying, "I know what they make at the Hanford site – it's a toilet paper factory. Every day my dad brings home two rolls of toilet paper in his lunch box!" This was the level of understanding at the time: each worker went out and did their job and did it well, pouring cement, building structures, machining equipment and tools, welding and so on knowing that it was for the safety of the US at wartime against the Nazis. Some I am sure smuggled home some government property too: toilet paper, screwdrivers, hammers, etc. The management at Hanford actually had a cover story that they would tell curious workers: that they were making a new innovative explosive called RDX.[34] The workforce was on a strict need-to-know basis about what was happening at Hanford in the 1940s. And very few of the workers needed to know.

The eager workers swarmed into this desolate place in massive numbers and many lived in army-style tents and barracks since there were not enough houses to put them in. There were 8 mess halls at Camp Hanford to feed the 50,000 workers at its peak. According to *Images of America: Richland Washington*, 2700 workers could be fed at once across all the mess halls. In a day 8000 pounds of coffee and 120 tons of potatoes were used. 7200 pies and 40,000 heads of lettuce were used per meal. 250 milk cows lived at the camp to supply milk for the daily breakfast. The government was building housing as quickly as it could and prefabricated housing was on the way. But many families and bachelors ended up

68

sleeping in sheds, barns, cars and the like. My grandparents were no different, both the McClearys from Butte and the Rawlings from New York (my mom's family) were shed livers when they first came to work at Hanford.

So, just as Pawn had heard in the 1930s in Detroit from Archie McCafferty that Butte was the place to go and make money, in the early 1940s he heard the same about Richland, Washington and the Hanford site from Earl Watts. Things in Butte were grim and the McCleary clan, 9 of them, loaded up in the 1936 Nash and headed to Richland. Little Jackie was just released from St. James Hospital with his broken leg, still in a cast, so he took up more than his share of room in the back seat. Sounds like Loretta Lynn lyrics to me. Pawn and Jean had no idea what was ahead for them in Washington but never afraid of the unknown off they all went 'over the hill', really the Rocky Mountains, to their new life further west of the Old Country.

When they arrived that night after 450 miles of hard driving over the mountains from Butte, Montana across Idaho to eastern Washington, Grandma Jean was at her wits' end, she'd smoked a dozen cigs to cope with the trip in the Nash. Pawn was an exceedingly reckless and fast driver and scared my grandmother to death with his driving skills or lack of skills, as it were. He always wanted or had a hot car and drove them fast day or night. The children fought and squabbled in the back seat across three states. When the Watts saw my family approaching in the Nash, one of them shouted, "Here come the McClearys!"

So they arrived in Kennewick, in the Columbia Basin in the desert of eastern Washington, and found the Watts' place in an orchard on Kennewick Avenue across from the golf course. The house the Watts lived in still stands across the street from the 3rd and 4th holes. When the rag-tag family of nine rolled up they found that the lodgings available were the Watts' apple packing shed out back. Highly resilient and hopeful to a fault my people unloaded from the Nash and made their first home in Washington in the apple shed in the Watts' back field. Fitting, Washington is the apple state after all.

While the Watts were living on Kennewick Ave., their dear dog, Pooch got sick. He had a big tumor on his neck and Earl and Margaret knew he needed to be put down. But Jim and Jean were on the way from Butte and they wanted Jean to see her dear friend Pooch before they put him to sleep. Jean hadn't seen the dog in the year and a half or two years that the Watts were in Washington ahead of the McClearys. He was in bad shape and was old for a big dog. When my family got to the Watts' place they exploded from the Nash, all nine of them, and Grandma Jean went to sit on the cement stoop at the back of the house. Probably for milky tea and a cigarette. Old Pooch marshaled the strength to walk to Jean and put his big head down on her lap. And he died. He had waited to see his old buddy Jean from Butte that treated him so well and just checked out with his head lying on the comfort of her familiar lap.

The next day, Pawn drove the Nash the ten miles out to Richland and north of the town to the Hanford Nuclear Reservation to sign up for work with the Carpenters. To work on the Hanford site in the 1940s, because of the top secret nature of the work, required a security clearance for everyone that would step on the property. Since Pawn was a Scottish native and a newly minted American citizen his government clearance took longer than most. The Watts family of six was gracious to let the McClearys camp out in the shed on the back of their property. All the McCleary and Watts kids were raised as family and had fun playing and getting into trouble on Kennewick Ave. just as they had at the 4 Mile in Butte.

Earl Watts was carpenter on the site or as most called it "The Area." The Area sounds like something from a science fiction movie but that is what we all (those of us that grew up here) called the Hanford site. I was in high school before I realized that it was kind of odd to ask the other kids, "Do your parents work at The Area?" - sounds like a Twilight Zone episode or Area 51 in Nevada where aliens and UFOs are occasionally spotted. But most school kids in the Tri-Cities which are Kennewick, Pasco and Richland had at least one parent working on the Hanford site from the 1940s through the late 80s. The Hanford workers ranged from blue collar construction workers to PhD engineers and scientists from around the country and the world.

The town of Richland, named after an early settler with the last name Rich (according to one account) was selected by the U.S. Army Corps of Engineers in 1940 because it was remote, in the middle of the desert in the southeast corner of Washington and it had the massively wide and strong Columbia River to cool the nine reactors that would eventually be built here.[35] Hanford also had hydroelectric power from the dams in the area, like Grand Coulee Dam, to fill the Hanford site's electric needs. Other sites in other desolate places were considered for this important and secret war effort but Hanford won out because of the river, the isolation of the location and the available electricity. The water pulled from the Columbia to cool the reactors would be treated and dumped right back into the river. Our leg of the Columbia then runs down through the Columbia Gorge that is the border between Washington and its southern neighbor Oregon, then flows through Portland and into the Pacific. During the boom years at Hanford there were over 50,000 workers housed at Camp Hanford in barracks and trailers and later the company town of Richland was erected to accommodate the workers and families that would be here long term. Some of us are still here. The James McClearys lived near the company town of Anaconda in Montana and under the thumb of the company in Butte so Richland was just another company town, and just like in the Old Country they followed the work and followed each opportunity. Like the Gaelic word spailpin, they followed the work – where-ever it was, that is where they went.

The work force that flocked to Hanford to build this plant were mainly white tradesmen, engineers, scientists and other support workers. The skilled trades represented were machinists and carpenters (my two grandfathers were these), ironworkers, millwrights, welders, etc. A smaller number of black workers were segregated from the white workers, in the Hanford photo archives there are pictures of the separate toilet facilities and eating areas for the black workers. Later DuPont brought more black workers from the south and placed them in houses in East Pasco. Or as old timers call it "eastside Pasco" On the job site, the white and black Americans were allowed to work together but not to socialize or mix in any other way.[36] The big Hanford contractors working for the government were DuPont, then General Electric: my grandpa Pawn worked for both.

Many of the hired hands came on their own and lived in the dormitories, barracks, others stayed in the tiny silver Airstream trailers set out in a little sandy grid on the desert amongst the sagebrush and rattlesnakes. At the construction peak there were 3000 trailers in the desert, and it gets hot – over 90 to 100 degrees for most of the summer. Eventually whole families arrived and Richland proper started to materialize.

When the powers that be chose the Camp Hanford site there three tiny community townships north of what is now Richland, right where they wanted to build the reactors and those folks where invited (strongly—with a letter from Uncle Sam that said their land was condemned and being seized by the government) to clear out immediately and make way for the project that they hoped would secure America's safety. That was all the land owners knew. Many of the farmers weren't allowed to bring in their last crop, but had to leave right then. Some were given three weeks to leave. Some were given financial compensation for their property, some were not. The townships of White Bluffs, Hanford, and old Richland were decimated and all that stands there today is the old schoolhouse. The Native American population along the Columbia River was ousted in the same way.

A fabulous feature of the Hanford site and of south-eastern Washington in general is the sand, the blowing sand. And not just a little but a lot and at high speeds. It can about sandblast your face off if you're not careful. They called these the "Termination Winds" in early Hanford days because after one sandstorm in the desert at Hanford many of the new hired hands that had just arrived from Oakland, Boston, Newark, Fargo or others parts unknown would 'drag up' or quit and got the next bus out of here. For some of the workers just arrived one sandblasting was more than enough. Luckily though, there were more workers arriving every day to take their place with the hammer, blowtorch, lathe or pencil. Hanford was the place to be in the 1940s to make big money just as Butte had been the place to be for miners in earlier times.

Pawn, Jean and the seven kids lived in the shed behind the Watts' house that sat on a half-acre lot across from the golf course and waited for Pawn's security clearance to come through. Hell, they were finally living by a golf course, but damn, they were living in a shed. Montana and the 4 Mile weren't looking half bad at this point. And they waited and waited and waited. There were 16 humans living on the Watts property; that's a lot of people and especially when 12 of them are kids. Pawn, who was getting nervous about how to feed the family and get them into a real house, heard a lead on work in a lumber mill in western Washington near a little town called Mossyrock.

Into the Nash they went again with their belongings and the kids, the eldest in the 7th or 8th grade, and headed west out of the desert and into the foothills of the Cascade Mountains. My dad told me when they made these journeys, with a car full of kids, Pawn would reach his limit with the fighting and squabbling coming from the back seat and reach back and 'fan' them. Being fanned was Pawn reaching back with his right arm while still driving (fast) with his left, and slapping with his fingers wide till he made contact a couple of times with someone or a couple of someones. This would usually calm the commotion coming from the 6 or 7 kids standing, sprawling and sitting on the back seat. Pawn was the disciplinarian and the kids didn't really mess with their dad. Grandma Jean was a soft touch had more trouble controlling the children and used the 'when your dad gets home' threat pretty liberally.

CHAPTER 8

MOSSYROCK, WASHINGTON USA - 1944

Mossyrock, Washington is about 200 miles or three and a half hours west of Richland driving Pawn-style in the Nash at the foot of the massive Cascade Mountain range. Southeastern Washington where the Tri-Cities (Richland, Pasco and Kennewick) are is an odd desert region of Washington State, sort of a banana belt. The rest of Washington and especially western Washington is green, lush with trees, mountains and old forests. Mossyrock, as the name implies, was like this and for Pawn and Jean this was more like the Old Country than the dry Columbia Basin wasteland of the Hanford site. Jean always loved travelling to places that reminded her of County Antrim or Harthill. Driving to Mossyrock was exciting for the kids and terrifying for my grandparents for a couple of reasons. Grandma Jean as usual was traumatized by Pawn's driving and the thought of him not finding work in this new place. Pawn was focused on getting work at that lumber mill but nervous just the same about feeding the family and finding some kind of shelter. Life in America was just as hard as the Old Country and at times of weakness he wondered if he and Jean should have come at all.

Pawn, Grandma Jean and all the kids sped closer to Mossyrock and the old Nash started to heave and chug in an odd way. The trip from Butte, Montana through the Rockies and the lesser mountain ranges of Idaho to Richland, Washington had taken a lot out of the old girl and now coming up to Mossyrock in 20 miles or so she was just done. Pawn coasted her over to the side on the grassy shoulder and Pawn and Jean got out and stood looking at the Nash Ambassador. All the kids bailed out and started horsing around and fighting and complaining on the side of the road. Pawn and Grandma had no idea what to do and struck up a cigarette – two of the last they had. About that time an old farm truck rolled up and stopped and out stepped Bill and Charlotte Schuler. They stopped to help the rumpled, Grapes of Wrath looking group that had materialized on the side of the road at the driveway to their farm.

Where Bill was short and stocky, Charlotte was tall and lanky. Rumor has it that Bill was not the most well groomed man in the world and wore the same set of work clothes for 20 years. But, appearances aside, they were the kindest, sweetest people and would be the third and final family in the McCleary lifelong friends club. They farmed produce and other crops that they needed to survive on their property outside of Mossyrock, Washington. Their house was small but cozy and they had lots of land with barns and outbuildings. Everything in Mossyrock was mossy and rocky and green like Ireland or Scotland and Grandma Jean especially loved that and the moist mountain air.

Standing out on the road, Bill invited them all to load into the back of his truck or walk alongside back to their place. Here they were: Pawn and Jean in their 30s, eldest kid Betty, 15 and 7 more kids down to Howie, age 2. They'd been in the car well over three hours; were hungry, tired and not so excited about this adventure at this point. Walking and riding onto the Shuler's property they had no idea what would happen to them. The Schulers invited them in for coffee and some sandwiches and promptly started to fall in love with this odd group of immigrants: the parents with the Scottish brogue and the kids cute as hell in various sizes, most with bright blue eyes and fair, freckled skin.

The Schulers put my family up in an outbuilding on their sizable and overgrown property. It was a shack with wooden planks for walls but plenty of daylight visible through them still and cold air seeping in. All this shack and shed living was making the kids think that the flat roofed house that they left on the 4 Mile in Butte, Montana was the lap of luxury. At this point, Pawn and Jean were wondering if the move to Washington State for the sure thing at Hanford was that great of an idea. But here they were and the Schulers were so kind and shared all they had. Everyone dragged their stuff into the shed and made up beds and makeshift living quarters as best they could. The kids made up their beds on the dirt floor. One of the McCleary girls briefly shared the spidery outhouse with a snake and then none of the girls would use the outhouse.

Pawn and Mr. Schuler towed the Nash to the farm and set about fixing it so Pawn could go find work at the saw mill. Through some fast talking and turning on of the charm, Pawn was hired at the saw mill. The old man was never afraid of hard work. Meantime, Jean and the kids were on the farm with the Schulers, trying to help out as they could in exchange for food and lodging. They all ate lots of fruit and vegetables. The two couples became fast and lifelong friends. The seven kids, raised in dry environments, had fun exploring, playing and discovering what was in the woods. The Cascade Mountains were beautiful and my dad always remembered the days in Mossyrock with fondness and appreciation at what the Schulers did for a car full of raggedy strangers down on their luck.

Jean kept in touch with Margaret Watts back in Kennewick and Pawn with the Hanford site to see when he could get on as a carpenter. Word finally came through and Pawn went to Richland to see if the carpenter job was for real. He would send for the family when he verified that it was solid. Grandma Jean and the kids waited expectantly for the good news. The work in the sawmill, while they were grateful for it, was hard work for low pay. The Hanford Nuclear site was supposed to be a goldmine if you got in early and worked hard. Some workers that got on in the 1940s would retire from here decades later. Both of my grandfathers did just that: the carpenter, James "Pawn" McCleary and my maternal grandfather Burdette "Bud" Rawlings, master machinist from New York worked at Hanford about 40 years each.

CHAPTER 9

RICHLAND, WASHINGTON USA -1944

Pawn sent for the family to come to Richland and after a long goodbye to their friends in Mossyrock, Jean and the kids arrived in Richland and could not believe their luck. Their dad not only had a carpenter's job on the Hanford site but had got a house. A prefab. Prefabricated housing was rolled into Richland in pieces and the homes slapped up quickly on a cement foundation to accommodate the growing population. Richland was divided up into neighborhoods with clumps of identical houses placed close together and offset at jaunty angles to keep the cookie-cutter neighborhoods interesting.

The house styles available were the 1 bedroom prefab, 2 bedroom prefab, 3 bedroom prefab, a precut, then A duplex, B duplex, C duplex, D house, F house and so on to M– then skip to the Q house and on to Z: the Alphabet houses. The Letter houses were more permanent than prefabs and came in an array of sizes and floor plans, none with more than 1500 square feet in the early days. The 1200 prefab houses erected between 1944-46 were designed for temporary living and had a shelf life of three years. Right now in Richland, some 68-70 years later, these prefabs are still there with people living in them. What was short term became permanent. My dad was incredulous and flabbergasted that the prefabs that sold for $1000 in the 1940s are now, in the 21st century selling for $80,000 or 100,000. They are the same houses with a little bit of lipstick and rouge added, in the form of shrubs and decks and oddball additions.

Pawn got his family a three bedroom, one bath prefab on the corner of Gratiot Street and Winslow across from the grade school, Marcus Whitman. They paid $12 a month rent to the government. The house was a sprawling 871 square feet and had a stylish flat roof - just like the 4 Mile. According to *The ABC Homes: the Houses that Hanford Built*, the dimensions of the three bedroom prefab were 27 ft. x 32 ft., for the **entire** house. Jim and Jean had one bedroom, 10 ft. x 10 ft.; the 4 girls, Bev, Betty, Anna, Dona had the other 8 ft. x 10 ft. room and the 3 boys, Jack, Howard and Tony had the third bedroom: just 7 ft. x 7 ft.[37] They had one full size bed in each room so the kids slept some with head on one end, some with head on the other.

My dad said the kicking and hitting and arguing with each other in the boys' bed was insane. They had a game called, "Where my arm falls I do not care" or substitute leg – you get the idea - and you had some real battles in the boys bed. Pawn would bust in a put a stop to it. "Jeeezus Christ man, what's wrong with you? Do you have shit for brains?" My aunt and uncle to this day say that the prefab on Gratiot was a palace, or the "Windsor Castle" they called it, to them after shed dwelling in Kennewick and Mossyrock. They thought they had arrived and were living in high style. The houses are cracker boxes and jammed onto a grid of blocks very close together with no trees or grass at that time. The Watts also lived in a prefab government house on Roberts Street and Jim Watts said that his family sat in their matchbox at that time musing, "I wonder what the poor people are doing tonight?"

Earl and Jim were both in the Carpenters and part of the job was to build and maintain this town full of 'Alphabet Houses'. A great perk of living in the government housing, all the maintenance and repair, even appliance maintenance, came free with your rent. So if something went wrong you just phoned up The Area and they sent someone out to trouble shoot and fix your problem right away. Pawn was on this maintenance team and got to know a lot of the transplant families while fixing their doors, windows, or whatever needed done to pull their little house back into order. Being from Scotland he got the nickname Scotty McCleary and the name stuck all through his Hanford career.

The town of Richland was laid out on a grid and all the larger, two story Alphabet Houses for the management and upper crust of Hanford were placed in the primo locations. For example, all the fancy Alpha Houses went beside the river. There was a hierarchy to the assignment of what house style you got based on your position on the site – sort of a World War II company town caste system. The prefabs were bottom of the barrel. My other grandfather who was a master machinist got a ranch house which was a cut above many of the other styles. It still stands in Richland now, 2012, as do most all that were built so quickly in the 1940s during those years of massive expansion for the secret project. Richland grew from 300 people on the farmsteads to 51,000 people in the space of two years.

My Grandma Jean, who had worked on her feet forever, and Margaret Watts both got jobs waitressing at the first café you saw as you entered beautiful downtown Richland. The new workers drove or rode the bus in on George Washington Way and dead ahead was the bus station café on the front facing the road, behind it was the Richland Community House that later had a restaurant. Jean and Margaret worked in both together for five years or so when Jean first arrived from Mossyrock. The café and then the restaurant hosted luncheons for dignitaries that came to town as there was no fancy hotel built yet. Mrs. Watts saved name tags from some of these visitors like nuclear program experts and luminaries like physicist, J. Robert Oppenheimer (father of the atom bomb), and leaders like Brigadier General Leslie Groves. The cafe was their hangout to eat and discuss the project. Hanford was a top secret operation highly important to the war effort and the crème de la crème showed up to help. Grandma Jean oddly found herself brushing elbows with the rich and famous while doing the most humble service work: Henry Ford, Ann Cody, Mr. Oppenheimer.

The Richland Community House downtown on George Washington Way was a large community center and along with the restaurant housed the Hi-Spot, which was a dance hall for teens on certain nights of the week. There was lots of posing, strutting and preening going on down at the Hi-Spot - and that was just the McCleary and Watts boys. There were other activities in the Community House too: bowling, pinball, a tavern. Much, if not all, of Richland was built to provide the basic services that the workers and their families needed for entertainment and leisure to occupy them in the off time from the plant – to keep them in Richland working.

Another place for families to pass the time in this desert outpost was the Richland Village Theater on Lee Ave around the corner from the Community House. The McCleary kids loved to go to the movies and it was affordable since each kid got 25 cents (or dad said 2 bits) a week allowance. To get into the Village was 12 cents per person and that left 13 cents - enough for "crumpets" meaning candy and popcorn and a drink. The only problem was that little brother Howie was always in trouble at home and didn't get his 25 cents for the week and so didn't have it for the movies on Saturday. When this happened, which was frequently, my dad would use his 25 cents to get both him and Howard into the show and forsake his crumpets so they both could see the movie. Jack and Howard were about seven and four years old at this time. Jack was sweet and generous always.

Some of the time, the McCleary kids didn't have an allowance at all and had to improvise to get into the movies at the Village. They'd all walk down to the Village movie house, the four sisters – Bev, Betty, Anna, Donna, from the prefab on Gratiot (pronounced Grat-chit by the locals) and now called Gray Street. This was really quite a hike and then they'd loiter outside the movie house. Along would come a girl friend from school that did have her 12 cents to get in and they'd persuade her to go on in, linger around in the lobby, then go to the "Ladies" and discreetly open the high window and leave. Then the McCleary sisters would boost each other up and in through the open window to the bathroom and sashay out to the lobby and into the movie. No crumpets for anyone on these trips. My 75 year old aunt exclaimed "Being poor was fun!" when she told me this story.

Later on Aunt Bev got a job working at the ticket booth at the Village, which was a great gig. Uncle Howie, only about four or five would come down and ask to see Bev at the booth to let him in. The ticket sellers would ask him, "Who are you and why do you need Bev?" and he'd say "I'm her sister!" They would laugh and laugh and Howie couldn't figure out what was so funny.

The Desert Inn

Around this time, the Desert Inn was built alongside the Columbia River in Richland for all the important Hanford visitors and dignitaries that came to town. It was a luxury hotel and restaurant with banquet facilities, a fur shop (of all things, in the desert), a candy store and a swimming pool. Grandma Jean went to work there waitressing and eventually worked her way up to head banquet manager. The Desert Inn was the hotspot in Richland and Grandma Jean showed up in her black and white waitress uniform ready to serve. She always accessorized with nice earrings, a broach and her signature cat eye glasses with jewels on them. She took great pride in her work and her work ethic was top notch.

When my grandmother was running the banquets at the Desert Inn, the Watts had the roof of their prefab on Roberts Street blow off. Earl and Margaret Watts were sleeping in their pigeon hole prefab bedroom during a big wind storm and suddenly they were gazing at the stars and their roof was in the middle of the street. Quite a few prefabs lost their roofs, they were just held on with L-brackets, in the early days. So the Area put the Watts family of six up in the Desert Inn for a month while a new roof was pasted on their prefab. Jim Watts said that my grandma would spoil them when they came down to the restaurant during that month. Grandma Jean would make them big ice cream sundaes for a special treat. My cousin said that Grandma Jean was so well known and respected by the high class visitors to the Desert Inn who called her "Jeanie," that she is still in the "Desert Inn Hall of Fame." Our grandma would carry eight plates of food up one arm and she moved very fast to get the job done, Uncle Howard said no-one else could do that.

Grandma Jean had 'the gift of the gab' and 'never met a stranger'; these are the clichés always used to describe her. Jean was a slightly built woman with fair skin and blue eyes but striking dark brows and hair and a squareish face. Everyone liked Jean McCleary and she could chat and entertain anyone with stories and jokes. Grandma Jean was outgoing with strangers but held her true feelings pretty close to the vest.

Up on the corner of Gratiot St. and Winslow St., the McClearys were living in the Windsor Castle. Pawn and Jean both worked every shift they could. Grandma Jean had a little trouble keeping all seven kids in line when she was home alone with them; she was a soft touch. Aunt Dona told me that their mother would tell them that when their father got home they were going to get it. And that was true, when Pawn walked in from working all day, Jean would give the report and he would get out the belt. The prefab was small and square with a front door and a back door directly opposite each other and the girls would start crying and wailing "No Daddy, No!" when they thought they'd get spanked and running out one door and back in the other. Then the boys would join in with the wailing and the running and it was a round robin of chaos. The belt was really an empty threat but it seemed to work. My aunt said it looked like a lunatic asylum with all the kids running and crying in and out of the house in circles, seven of them.

Pawn was a frugal man. He had lived through very hard times, had to fight for everything that he and his family had and would not stand for wastefulness. The prefab had a little stand up shower with a flimsy plastic curtain in the corner of the tiny bathroom; they were like what you would see in a recreational vehicle today. On shower day each McCleary got into the little closet of a shower, was allowed to turn the water on to wet down their body only for a couple of seconds, then had to turn the water off. Next they soaped down their body and hair while freezing their little asses off in there shivering. Only then could they turn on the water again for a fast rinse, no languishing under the hot water and … boom, off went the water and they got out.

In his old age, Pawn could still tell you exactly where contaminated, irradiated items from his day were buried on the Hanford reservation. In those times, the dangerous "crapped up" items were buried in the sand way out on the Site, a 550 square mile reservation. Some of the items he talked about were giant cranes (and not the birds) laid down on their side and buried in the sand or dump trucks buried like a dog's bone, not just hammers and screwdrivers and tool belts. He said he'd been in the United Mineworkers or some other labor union for 50 years and didn't understand the lack of support for the union that he saw in America as opposed to the Old Country. He wrote some strongly worded letters to the newspaper editor and to GE in favor of the union at Hanford. Uncle Howard said his dad was not an educated man, he only went to school till fourteen as did Grandma Jean, but was very smart and direct. The Union lawyer remembers my grandpa for his strong voice in the Carpenters Union and for the 25 one-arm pushups that he could still do as an old man.

The Watts and the McClearys were still close and socialized when the fathers weren't working out at the Area or in Richland doing the carpenter work on government houses and when the mothers weren't working: Grandma Jean at the Desert Inn and Margaret Watts by this time working at the Hanford site laundry. The Watts and McCleary kids ran in little gangs of threes and fours through the company town of Richland. New Year's Eve was a special celebration for the two families since the early 1930s when they were neighbors in Butte. The Watts were from Irish ancestry that moved to Scotland like the McClearys. Strike up the bagpipe for the ancient Scottish festival of Hogmanay! (pronounced Hug manney). The two families brought this tradition from the 4 Mile in Butte to Richland with them. It's a Scottish New Year's Eve ritual in which, at the stroke of midnight, one bursts out of their house like a man afire and runs to the nearest neighbor's and through their front door. No knocking, of course. Once inside they did a jig or sang a song or recited a poem and the startled homeowners rewarded them with a treat and they dashed with their prize out the back door and on to the next house. This mayhem went on as each of the 20 or so people, adults and kids, terrorized the neighborhood on New Year's Eve. Part of the tradition is that it is preferred that the first person to cross your threshold be a tall, handsome, dark man – but at least in the McCleary clan it was mostly slight, white and freckly invaders busting in the door. Jean and Margaret trained the neighbors to expect this on New Year's Eve and day and thus the milque-toast town of Richland, Washington, had some Old Country tradition introduced. These days it would never work and you'd get shot at the first house, when the owners reacted to a home invasion. My dad always said on New Year's Eve that Pawn, Grandma Jean and Margaret Watts would sing all the old songs from Ireland and Scotland and the ladies would cry and cry. Then they'd start hugging and wailing, "I love you Margaret," "I love you Jean" - every New Year's Eve. They sang "Mrs. Murphy's Chowder" and "Timothy Kelly" amongst other Old Country folk standards and funny songs.

All the Watts and McCleary kids were trained to address adults formally. Howard, however, was another story: he was a bit of a brat and a spirited handful. When he was little he called Margaret, Margaret - once. Mrs. Watts told him to call her Mrs. Watts and not Margaret. Howie didn't agree with that request and stuck his tongue out at Mrs. Watts. Mrs. Watts said, "Howard McCleary don't stick your tongue out at me!" Howie hesitated for effect, then turned and directed his little butt at her and farted in her direction. Not a dummy, Howard then took off running as fast as he could. Mrs. Watts chased him down at top speed and grabbed him. Back at the Watts yard she lit up Howards butt with her spanking strap. Howie, outraged, screamed and cried "I'm gonna tell my dad that you spanked me!" and Margaret yelled back, "Not if I tell him first…!" The McClearys and Watts kids really were raised as siblings by the four parents and I am certain that Howie had it coming and that Pawn was in favor of the switching by Mrs. Watts. Pawn spanked Howie when he got home too, just to make sure he got the point.

After elementary school at Marcus Whitman my dad started to hang out at the bowling alley "Atomic Lanes" with Uncle Howard in tow. Jack's first obsession was playing the pinball machines but that took money so he soon gravitated to the man's world of shooting pool. He was ten years old. Along with him and Howie was his buddy Jerry Yates. Jerry Yates was my dad's best childhood friend and close with him until the day he died. So his buddy was there when he discovered that he had a natural talent for shooting pool. My dad practiced every day at the bowling alley, this was in the early 1950s, and started challenging grown men to games. My dad was very small and sweet looking like a little boy doll with a freckled nose so these pool hall guys probably thought, "Oh how cute, this little shit is challenging me to a game of pool – I'll show him how it's done." Dad would promptly clear the table. His buddy Yates said he could take 15 cents and turn it into 15 dollars in a short time. Then he and Yates would split the winnings, because they'd both chipped in their lunch money from Marcus Whitman for the wager. Or my dad would bet on difficult trick shots, sink them, and collect that way too. Jack graduated from the bowling alley to the local pool halls in Richland. Jim Watts said he only saw Jack lose a pool game about two times, just because he wasn't paying attention. My dad was a pool shark and a pool hustler as a kid and put the hurt on a lot of grown men's wallets for many years, separating them from the money they made out on the Hanford site. They say my dad could have gone on the pro pool circuit, he was that good.

In the Richland school days my dad and his buddy Yates and Howard ran wild and got in lots of trouble, with their parents and the public at large. Yates says they were the three amigos. When dad and Yates were fourteen they decided to follow the Columbia High School Bombers (indeed, the Richland mascot is a bomber plane) to the State Basketball Championship playoff game… in Seattle! So they hitchhiked, without telling their parents, from Richland to Seattle, 225 miles away. They were two small town 8th grade boys determined to get to the Hec Ed (Clarence S. "Hec" Edmundson) Pavilion. It was an ambitious journey and by the time they got there they were shell-shocked by the weirdness of some the people who'd picked them up and of the big city itself. Then they found the game, watched and had to hitchhike home—it took a very long time. Not their most inspired plan. When he staggered home from his football odyssey, my dad found that no one ever knew he was gone. Uncle Howard did the same thing a year later when he was twelve and no one knew he was gone from Richland either. Yates said he and Jack were raised like brothers; Yates spent a lot of time amongst the McClearys.

My dad and Howard and their friends hunted in the Columbia Basin for small birds, ducks and geese while they were growing up. Jim Watts has written his own book, The Animal,[39] about his hunting and other adventures in Richland at this time. As he tells in his book, there was an overly enthusiastic game warden in the area during those years, whose sole obsession was catching these young, hot-shot greasers poaching or otherwise breaking a gaming law out in the boonies. He took his job very seriously and stalked the Watts and McCleary boys and their friends for years chasing them down, writing them tickets and confiscating their weapons. The local boys and the warden had a pretty good game of cat and mouse going for a long time. The Columbia Basin in eastern Washington is a great place to hunt with all kinds of birds and small game and bodies of water. It was a good diversion for the Richland boys.

My dad was a little guy but a huge smart ass and got in quite a few fights with his classmates and neighbors. There was one guy in 8th grade that really bugged him and my Dad started calling him "Ears." This fellow did have some very prominent ears but he was quite a bit larger than my dad. Down at the Hi-Spot dance hall little Jack kept teasing this guy about his ears saying, "Hey Ears, when you go under the underpass you'd better pull those ears in or you'll get stuck." This sent Ears into a rage and he and Jack fought. I guess my dad won the fight this time and though he was short in stature he was not short on attitude or guts.

Uncle Tony and the Watts boys started some sort of a riot over at a grocery store at the Richland Y or Wye. The Richland Y was a little crossroads at the river between Richland and Kennewick and had a bar, Wild Bill's Grocery store and a drive-in movie theater. The boys went in Wild Bill's grocery and one of them shouted "Wild Bill eats shit!" over the loudspeaker. All hell broke loose and they fought with Wild Bill and the butcher with his meat cleaver, then more kids came to join the fight. Finally the cops came. It was a true free-for-all in the McCleary sense. This is how the teen boys stayed busy living in the middle of the desert just after World War II and into the Cold War years.

The McClearys, with Pawn working on the site and Grandma Jean in charge of banquets at the Desert Inn, finally started to get ahead and have a little extra money. When they had it, Pawn and Jean would go buy staples like flour, sugar, potatoes, and the like, and travel to deliver them to the Schulers in Mossyrock. All through the years they went to visit about once a year and took food supplies to repay Bill and Charlotte Schuler for their kindness when they first came to Washington. These visits were great fun for the adults and kids. Howie remembers camping with the Schulers kids and grandkids – a brood of about 25 counting McClearys and Schulers. Uncle Howard had a crush on Rosie, the Schulers niece who was a fire lookout in the forest around Mossyrock. Rosie had a jerk boyfriend named Ike and Howard vowed to himself to return to Mossyrock when he was grown and kick Ike's ass. Howard vowed to kick a lot of asses over the years. There are black and white pictures of the trips that show the two families having a great time camping in the forest around Mossyrock. Pawn would speed over to Mossyrock in his orange Mercury Turnpike Cruiser with three of my cousins, Jeff, Tod and Kyle who Pawn called "the Three Chickenitos" in the back, pinned by the velocity.

Pawn, Grandma Jean and the kids did a lot of car travelling to see America and Canada. Some family from the Old Country lived in Eastern Canada by this time. Pawn and Jean had a different ideas about what travel was all about. Pawn liked to drive fast and get somewhere, Jean liked to go slow, stop and admire the scenery, especially if it was green and woodsy. There wasn't a scenic viewpoint that Jean didn't like. On one of these car trips they stopped, Jim, Jean and at least five kids at a roadside café to have a cup of tea and a soda for the kids. Jean went in and sat at the counter and ordered her tea and lit up a cigarette. When she spoke the brogue was very apparent and people asked her where she was from. Grandma started talking and getting to know the waitresses behind the bar and some other people at the counter, Jim and the kids had their tea and soda in a booth.

After a bit Pawn said "Load up!" and the kids all headed to the car. He signaled Grandma Jean that they were ready to go and headed outside with the kids. In the Mercury, they all waited, and waited, and waited. Pawn sent one of the little ones in to get their mother. No luck, Grandma was still talking and didn't come. Another kid was sent into the café to say if she didn't come dad said that they were leaving. Still no Jean. Pawn got out of the car opened the trunk, took Jean's square, well-worn suitcase out and sat it on the sidewalk in front of the parking spot. He got back in the car, fired it up and off they went down the road. The kids were shocked, speechless that he would leave their mother at a roadside café so far from home.

Pawn kept driving and driving along. Finally the kids broke down and said "Dad, why did you leave Mom?" "Dad, what is going to happen to Mom?" Pawn muttered something and kept driving. The five kids in the back got more agitated and frantic. The crying started, the wailing, "Dad, you gotta go back and get mom!" "Mom's gonna die if you don't go back!" from all the McCleary kids who were quite fond of their mother. After a bit, the hysteria hit a peak and Pawn pulled off the road and made a U-turn back the way they'd come. Quite a while had passed since they'd left Jean at the café and the kids thought she'd be mad as a hornet that Jim had left her. They were anticipating quite a battle when mom got in the car. Pulling up to the roadhouse their eyes bulged to see mother's suitcase sitting on the curb where Dad had put it. Pawn pulled into the same spot, got out and went in the café. Grandma Jean was still perched up on a swivel stool at the lunch counter, sipping her milky tea, smoking and entrenched in conversation about someone's family in the mountain town. Pawn walked up and stood beside her, she looked over, smiled and said, "Aye, are you all ready to go now?" Pawn nodded and they left the café. Jean had no idea that she'd been left behind in the mountain diner because of the gift of the gab that came so naturally to her.

In 1950, when my Aunt Beverley was nineteen, she was crowned Miss Richland. Beverley McCleary was one of the great beauties of the time as well as an outstanding athlete. That year the Hanford site was a focus of attention in the US because they'd raised a great amount of money for the War Bonds, this brought assorted dignitaries to visit the site and Richland. The Cold War threat was uppermost in everyone's minds and Hanford was a plutonium factory for the war machine. Government, science and even Hollywood visitors stayed at the Desert Inn where Grandma Jean was banquet manager. One of the visitors was movie star Kirk Douglas and when he arrived Aunt Beverley, as Miss Richland, was assigned as his social escort for his stay in Richland. We have great pictures of Kirk Douglas presenting a bouquet to my aunt and holding her gloved hand while looking into each other's eyes. There are also photos of Bev out by the pool at the Desert Inn with a famous wrestler. Bev sporting a modest swimsuit, sexy high heels and a Miss Richland sash and the stocky wrestler in a skimpy man's, Jack LaLanne-style swimsuit. In one photo, Aunt Bev is squeezing his bicep while he flexes in the sunlight, his oily body glistening. Beverley was tall and lovely with dark brunette hair, fair skin with a dimple in her cheek and bright blue eyes. I have old film of her from riding on the back of a big old convertible in a parade wearing a stylish big brimmed hat and tailored suit and waving her gloved hand to the crowd. My aunt represented Richland well and is still remembered by old timers for her exceptional beauty. I get the feeling she was the Jackie Kennedy of Richland in those days: brunette, stylish, mysterious, beautiful.

Uncle Jim

In 1950, Grandma Jean's mother Rachel McAleese, who'd raised Uncle Jim from two months old, died in Harthill, Scotland. Grandma Jean flew home to Harthill for the first time in more than 20 years, since they had sailed away to Canada. This would be the first time that she saw her son James McCleary since he was two months old. The family saw plenty of pictures as Jim grew up in Scotland, when to school, joined the Royal Air Force when he was very young, but this was the first in-person reunion with her eldest, longed for child.

Grandma Jean had a ticket on one of those huge silver planes that look so bloated it's a wonder they could fly at all. Grandma boarded the flying whale with her cigarettes and tea and off she went to Scotland. It was a three-day flight in long segments and she could while away the hours as long as there was someone to talk to; God Bless whoever sat beside her for that long trip. Grandma Jean always dressed very stylishly with head wraps, cat eye glasses and flats. She wanted to look good to meet her son and show off her American self to her family. Jean and Aunt Lizzie are the only Hunters to come to America from that generation.

The first meeting between mother and son was bittersweet. Jim was cool, resentful and aloof at the reunion with his mother that left him behind 21 years earlier in 1928. He felt betrayed by his family in America, though several attempts had been made to bring him over through the years. Jim was a little formal and stoic by nature anyway. Grandma Jean did break through and convince Jim to come to America to meet his family and possibly live in Richland. Jim looked a lot like 'the old man' at that same age: fair skin, blue eyes, handsome, muscular and physically fit. He had just lost his grandmother, who was the only mother he remembered. Uncle Jim and Grandma Jean flew to the west coast of America on July 10, 1950 landing in Pasco, Washington and then home to Richland, the town across the river.

When young, dashing 21 year old Jim McCleary arrived in Richland Washington in 1950 it was akin to an international incident. It was written up in the Tri-City Herald. He was a sensation, a foreigner, handsome, light on his feet and part of the already numerous and some might say notorious McCleary family on Gratiot Street. Uncle Jim from the Old Country had Scottish ways, a Scottish brogue and arrived with a flash of style. Jack, Howard and all the other McCleary kids were so curious about their long lost brother that they had heard about and envisioned all their lives. He did not disappoint. Jim McCleary was an Arthur Murray dance instructor in Scotland and could do all the dances: Scottish Fling, rumba, samba, all the ballroom dances. Arthur Murray was a chain of dance studios around the world and to teach there was a pretty slick job. Jim showed off his dancing to the riveted kids in Richland. Jim was a little older, 21 or 22, so all the single girls in town were quite interested in him too. Uncle Jim had served in the Royal Air Force in Scotland when he was very young - in his portrait from the Air Force he looks about 14 years old – in WWII. Jim was a soccer star in Scotland and thought he'd be able to further his budding soccer career in America. Much to his chagrin and disappointment when he got here, he found out that American football was entirely different, that it was not soccer at all. After a while he found out about a professional or semiprofessional soccer team in Seattle: the Seattle Sunny Jims and went there to play for them for a time.

Jim had grown up very poor in Scotland in the mining village and when he got to Richland and saw how all his siblings, seven of them, had been living he was envious. Although the living arrangements in the Windsor Castle were cramped and austere to put it mildly, he had to bunk in as the fourth boy in the boys 7 x 7 foot bedroom with the one full sized bed. Uncle Tony was 15, Jack was 8 and slept at one end: Uncle Jim was 21 and Howard, 5 and they slept at the opposite end. The 8 legs were all tangled up in the middle - yet it seemed a lot better to Uncle Jim than how he'd lived in Harthill all those 21 years. They had still lived in miner's housing all through his life. Here began a bit of jealously and resentment. Maybe it was because Richland was such a sweet 1950s, company town where everything was easy and entertaining for the Hanford worker families even if you were poor. Maybe it was just the fact that he'd missed so much camaraderie and family togetherness and felt left out and left behind. Whatever it was when my grandparents finally, after years of fretting, saving hard won money, and longing for him, sent for Uncle Jim and he came, it was not all roses and sunshine.

My dad was nine years old and for him it was the greatest thing ever, to have this swashbuckling foreigner come to town and have him be your brother for God's sake! What luck. The prefab on Gratiot and Winslow was on the corner right across from Marcus Whitman Elementary School and all the kids in the neighborhood gathered there to watch Jim McCleary with the soccer ball. His handling skills were like nothing the kids in Richland had seen before. My dad said a pack of neighborhood kids, about 20 of them, in all sizes would oppose Jim and he'd try to work the ball down the field with a wall of kids protecting the goal and guarding him. Using all his Old Country skills he'd kick it over their heads and pick it up on the other side of all the kids and score in the makeshift goal. The kids would go wild, shouting and clapping with amazement. Jack was pretty proud that this was his big brother.

Hunting for the teen and older boys in Richland was popular and the elder Watts boys took Uncle Jim out hunting for small birds in the local hunting hotspots. Once they got out there and scouted out the area, Uncle Jim started blasting the seagulls out of the sky. Jim Watts said "Hey you can't shoot seagulls in America, it's illegal!" Uncle Jim very surprised said in his Scottish brogue, "I shot them and et them all the time in the Old Country." Watts said, "You did? How did they taste?" Jim replied in thick brogue, "Aye... they were pretty good, that is once you got the first mouthful down." Uncle Jim had a lot to learn about the American way of life.

Howard was Grandma Jean's baby and kind of spoiled so Uncle Jim picked on him quite a bit. Howard told me he vowed then to kick his brother Jim's ass when he grew up. There are 15 years between the two. At this time, Beverley one of the elder sisters, had a job at the Hanford site and was paying rent at the house, so Pawn and Grandma Jean thought she should have a room to herself. That meant the boys room became Bev's room and the four boys including 21 year old Jim had to sleep out in the living room on the couch and floor. The prefabs were beyond small and had tiny yards. The nearest neighbors were the McMillians, whose daughter Bonnie is a family friend even now. Once the McClearys made a friend of you, they never let loose.

Physical strength was revered and respected and Pawn led his kids in "Feats of Strength" they called it - for friendly competition, entertainment and to exercise the sometimes bored kids. The Feats of Strength were pull ups on the ever-present pull up bar, for boys and girls of course. The house on Gratiot had a pull up bar connected to the house right outside the back door. Going Through the Broom was a series of fancy steps and turns while passing a horizontal broom stick under your feet, and was another regular exercise. I could have one of my aunts or my uncle demonstrate for me but they are all in their 70s and 80s and I don't want one of them laid up on my account. Pushups were part of the Feats repertoire and Pawn could do many one armed pushups and pullups so he was the man to beat. There was a broad jump contest and Pawn had his kids trying to jump an 8 ft. long piece of plywood lying on the ground. My uncle told me that Pawn could jump it like a jackrabbit, no problem. The Feats of Strength included running races, arm wrestling and other competitions. Feats of Strength went on for years, when the family lived in Richland proper and later in West Richland. No sexism here, the girls all competed right in with the boys.

All through Pawn's life physical power had served him well, made money for him, established his place in communities, and entertained lots of people so his kids were brought up to be as strong and tough and proud as they could be. One of my beautiful and stylish aunts beat up a boy at a high school dance in the 50s that surely deserved it and probably never forgot it. I imagine it was all fair skin, brunette hair, corsage and fluffy chiffon flying into the heat of battle. One of my other aunts wanted to ride a motorcycle owned by a boy at school and he was willing to let her drive his bike but was secretly more interested in her than teaching her to drive it.

So she drove the motorcycle with the boy on the back through the desert and was having a grand time until the boy sitting behind her started to get a little handsy and cop a feel of her chest from behind. Outraged, my aunt hauled off and elbowed the boy in the face with her left elbow while holding on to the handle bars with her right hand. She lost control of the motorcycle and there was a huge crash, she was launched over the handle bars and Mr. Hands flew and landed in the sand and sagebrush. All the pull-ups and pushups came in handy when she needed elbow power. My aunt, amazingly was not hurt at all but the boy came out with a broken arm and had to wear a cast and a sling while it healed. Word got around Richland about what happened and the boy was humiliated while our McCleary girl was shocked at the boy's brazenness and nerve but was pleased with herself for defending her own honor.

When eager suitors came around to take one of my aunts on a date or just visit them at the house, Pawn would run the boys through some paces and only the mentally and physically strong survived the first visit. He'd hand each boy his metal lunchbox from the Hanford site and have them stand in front of him holding their arms out to the side, imagine Jesus on the cross, that position, but with a lunchbox held in one hand. And that lunchbox is heavy, my brother has it and its more like a homemade metal piecebox than a modern lunchbox made in a factory; the handle is a heavy piece of thick wire twisted crudely in a loop. Pawn would time them and see how long they could hold that metal box out like that without caving in and letting it come down. Word on the street is my Uncle Charlie held it out for 6 minutes which is the all-time record. He's in his 70s now. So Pawn gave all young fellows a trial by fire before taking one of his four daughters out or even talking to them at length. The old man could hold the lunchbox in his hand on the extended arm for 16 minutes.

Down in Columbia Park that runs alongside the Columbia River between Richland and Kennewick there was a gas station called the "Tex-AK- o" by Uncle Jim and he got a job pumping gas and washing windows there. Uncle Jim had a childhood sweetheart back in Scotland named Helen that he had left behind and he missed her very much. Uncle Jim had the same sarcastic, dry, witty sense of humor that my dad was known for. Jim Watts said Uncle Jim and my dad, Jack were the most alike in mannerisms and personality of all the McCleary kids.

One of Uncle Jim's more spectacular stunts was a dive off the top of the Green Bridge (is what we called it) that spanned the Columbia between Kennewick and Pasco. This was truly insane since he climbed to the highest peak, posed and did a perfectly executed swan dive with arms extended and chest out into the cold, deep Columbia about 70-100 feet below. There were no dams upstream in the Columbia at this time and it was moving right along. All the kids thought this was incredible and all the adults thought it incredibly stupid, a good way to get killed.

That Green Bridge, in the 1940s, 50s and 60s separated the white town of Kennewick from the town of Pasco where most of the African Americans lived. There was a sign on the green bridge that said all Blacks must be out of Kennewick and back into Pasco by dark each night. The Hanford contractors had brought 15,000 African Americans up to work at the Area from the southern United States and they lived in Eastside Pasco segregated from the whites.

Pawn and Grandma Jean saved all the money they could from their jobs while living on the corner of Gratiot and Winslow. They were still working their asses off at the Hanford site and the Desert Inn and raising their large and lively family. The older sisters, Betty and Bev and Anna, moved out and got jobs in Richland. The younger ones were still at home, Jack, Howard, Dona and Tony when my grandparents finally had enough money to move out of the government housing.

CHAPTER 10

WEST RICHLAND - 1950

Jim and Jean searched around the area for the best deal on land and found it in what is now called West Richland but then was three little rural towns near each other. My grandparents bought ten acres of the scrubby, dry, sage-brushy, Russian olive tree dotted property so typical in eastern Washington from Old Man Hunt. The land is located on Ranch Road in West Richland and is on the dreaded flood plain, but at the time Pawn bought it there had only been one flood in 1938 according to Old Man Hunt, the owner of all the land around there. The Yakima River runs through this area on its way to join the mighty Columbia River just a little further down. The ten acres were purchased and Pawn set about building a workshop on the corner of Ranch Road and 46th street. A short while later he added a house onto the shop and James, Jean and the kids moved out to West Richland in 1950. Finally a house with a pitched roof; unlike Butte at the 4 Mile and the prefab in Richland. The years of carpentry paid off.

In the new West Richland house they had the luxury of a bathtub, not just a little shower, but Pawn only allowed one inch of water in the tub for bathing. I wouldn't be surprised if there was a one inch mark taped off in the tub with his carpenter's level to make sure no-one exceeded the water mark. And the cheese cutter. Pawn was a man that loved sharp cheddar cheese for a cheese sandwich and did not want it wasted or used wantonly. It sat out on the Formica table in the kitchen on a marble slab under a glass cover and if you wanted cheese you cut off a slab with the cheese slicer and carefully put the cover back on. It was not an option to leave the cover off and let it get hard or to cut it any other way than in a straight line with the cutter. Those who did not comply with these guidelines would rue the day they ate the McCleary cheese. A pot of boiled potatoes was usually on the stove for anyone that was hungry, family and guests alike, and Pawn liked his with lots of butter and pepper. Pawn would pepper his spuds till they had a black crust on top. Pawn and Grandma Jean drank what they called English tea, black tea with about half milk. My grandparents made a signature dish Skilllagalerry: a watery stew with ground meat, water, carrots, onions, turnips, rutabagas, potatoes and cabbage. After adding the cabbage the whole house smelled like old dirty gym socks.

Growing up in small town Washington in the 1950s my dad, the pool shark, ran around town mostly with Yates and Howard. My dad and Howie were the youngest in a long line of children and by that point their parents "put them on automatic," as my dad would say. They didn't really have to answer to anyone. In the hot summer, which in Richland is in the 90s and 100s, all the kids gathered at the public pool, called The Big Pool, to swim and left their bikes in the bike rack. The Big Pool was at the bottom of a hill and the bike racks were out of sight of the pool and loaded with bikes, dozens of them with no locks. In the 50s no one locked up their bike. Jack and Howard each plucked out a bike and rode like hell up the hill on it. To get home from Richland to West Richland was a long way, Howard and Jack had hitchhiked the seven miles into town earlier in the day.

Once you hit the Yakima River Bridge you were almost to West Richland proper. They rode the hot bikes up on the bridge, then Jack and Howard heaved the stolen bikes over the rail and into the river and walked the rest of the way home. They did this a lot. One year the Yakima River got really low and under the bridge into Richland there was a graveyard of stolen bikes from the McCleary boys. For years people fished off that bridge and were forever hanging up their lures and tackle on the damned stolen bikes beneath the Yakima River. Once in a while if the bikes were really nice, they rode them home and quickly stripped them down of any identifying accessories and repainted the bike with fancy swirls and details. Then they told Pawn and Grandma Jean that they got the new bikes from the Davies boys, the Davies boys were home doing the same and telling their parents that they got the new bikes from the McCleary boys. So they were petty crooks. Over 60 years later, Uncle Howard says that they were "chicken-shit bastards" for doing that to the other kids.

Pawn and Jean and the kids left at home took over a restaurant in West Richland to make some money on the side. It was called Lindy's Café and its slogan was "Sho 'Nuf Fried Chicken" and served, as you would guess, fried chicken and other café food. The McClearys owned and ran the café for a couple of years with Howard and Jack peeling potatoes and working the counter.

Aunt Dona remembers Pawn breaking 90 mph in the Merc taking her, Jack and Howie to school one day, Pawn late for work at Hanford. Uncle Howie says Pawn was the worst driver and always said that he was the best. Howard thought everyone drove like that. The old man would approach stop signs and slam on the brakes, the car would lunge forward. Pawn squealed tires around corners, hit railroad tracks at high speed, got airborne and landed with more squealing tires. My dad and Aunt Dona were terrified in the back and Howie on the floorboards crying. Pawn's passing technique was getting right up on the ass of the car ahead, then out and zip right back in front. Uncle Howie says that Pawn's famous shortcuts amounted to being lost on most McCleary family vacations.

In 1955 when Elvis Presley exploded onto the scene, Jack was fifteen and Elvis was the coolest man anyone had ever seen. Dad said that it was a thrilling time that he would never forget. My dad also told me that he and a friend were speeding down a long straight road in Richland one day, his friend was driving way too fast and they were yukking it up and having fun. Suddenly in the road they spotted a cardboard box up ahead. Like teens would do they said to each other, "hit the box" "no don't hit the box" back and forth. They thought it would be pretty amazing to smash that box like a pancake going about 50 miles per hour down the residential street. At the last minute the driver swerved and they sailed past the medium sized cardboard box. As they did, they saw movement and a little toddler popped his head out of the box. There was a baby in the box in the middle of the road!

Uncle Howard had earned quite a reputation for fighting in Richland and was in trouble all the time: car wrecks, teeth knocked out, arrests and the like. They were living in West Richland which was known as the horsey, hickish rural area outside of town and not as cool as the company town of Richland with its row houses. There was a guy of Bev's age who was the toughest guy in Richland at the time and everyone was scared of him. He was quite a ladies man and had some illegitimate kids here and there and enjoyed knocking women around. He was sitting up at the bar in the local tavern one day holding court and discussing Miss Richland 1950, Bev McCleary and her beauty. His cronies were all agreeing that she was quite a package and then the tough guy ringleader said scornfully, "She's a McCleary, they are all just West Richland trash." Uncle Howard who was at least five years this guy's junior happened to be sitting at the bar that night too. He heard what the guy said and calmly walked up to him, tapped him on the shoulder, and when he turned stated, "I'm Howie McCleary." And without further ado proceeded to beat the hell out of the toughest guy in town in spectacular fashion. This became stuff of legend, since Howard was so much younger and unknown and it humiliated the other guy so much. After that it was a known fact: you say something in Richland about the McClearys you'd be dispatched by Howard sooner or later. As my dad would say, "the McClearys are gonna clan up on ya."

In 1958, Jim Watts, the little boy from the 4 Mile in Butte was the Student Body President of the local junior college, Columbia Basin College and invited none other than Mrs. Eleanor Roosevelt to the college to speak at the lecture series. Jim said the reason that she accepted was that the eastside of Pasco was the worst ghetto in the western United States at the time and she wanted to see it in person. East Pasco had high rent and unsanitary, substandard conditions for the black workers and their families. Jim and her driver escorted her all around the Columbia Basin which has many hydroelectric dams that she wanted to see as well. Construction workers repelled down the dam to speak to her and get her autograph. Jimmy Watts spent two days with Mrs. Roosevelt and became quite friendly with her and attended the local Democratic reception given in her honor. I include this information because it is historically significant and surprising because Jim Watts was kicked out of two local high schools permanently, one for riding a motorcycle down the hallway inside the school and the other for dropping a typewriter out of the 2nd story window. Then he managed to get into college and become the ASB President. So Jim Watts securing this historic visit was all the more amazing.

My Uncle Jim left Richland and went northwest to Seattle to play soccer for the Sunny Jims. Jim didn't blend in well with the family and had some Old Country habits that didn't fly in the New World. For example, he ordered his sisters around and would incessantly tap the side of his teacup with his spoon for the girls to refill his tea and that sort of thing. They did not find that charming at all, said Aunt Betty. He always seemed to be jealous and bitter over the time he'd missed with the family and all that they had: which wasn't much. Pawn was hard on Uncle Jim too as he was all the boys, telling him "Can't you get rid of that accent, man? You're an American now."

Alaska

Uncle Jim came back from Seattle and went on a family vacation with Pawn and Jean and the younger kids to Canada. They dropped him off in Vancouver BC and from there he went to Seward, Alaska and worked on the red salmon fishing boats in the Bearing Sea and as a longshoreman driving forklift. He made a ton of money for the time, the 1950s, about $35,000 per year; Pawn made $6,000 per year at Hanford. Jim built a house in Alaska but also started to drink quite heavily – not a good plan if you have McCleary and Hunter blood coursing through your veins. Uncle Jim also fancied himself a riverboat gambler and lost most of his money gambling. He married two Native Alaskan girls, one after the other, during this period and those marriages failed because as Aunt Betty and my dad both said "those Eskimo girls could out-drink him!" I have a photo of Jim in a 50s style swimsuit and one of his wives in a modest ladies suit posing on some craggy rocks beside the sea. Jim McCleary was a handsome and fit man. He was a bit of a loner and a wayward soul – but he was always adventurous.

In Alaska, my uncle worked gathering up mountain goats for the circus for a man called "Goathead Williams" on the Kenai Peninsula about 30 or 40 miles from Seward. Jim was Goathead's helper; it took two people to catch the mountain goats in snares and bring them down out of the cliffs. Their base camp was on the beach and a supply ship came regularly to pick up the animals to take them away to zoos or circuses around the world. Uncle Jim and Goathead climbed 3,000 to 4,000 ft. straight up a sheer wall of bedrock with packs on their back and set rope snares on the skinny goat trails that had been carved in the cliffs over hundreds of years. They camped, tied off on the rock face, and waited to catch one of the 400 lb. beasts by the foot. When they did, Goathead would lariat the mountain goat's head with a lasso and Jim would do the same and they would hog-tie the legs and start to bring the animal down. It sometimes took two days to get to the bottom; Jim and Goathead would alternate dallying off and moving the animal down. They'd tie off and sleep if necessary with the goat part of the tied off camping party. In four months' time, Uncle Jim and Goathead trapped and removed seven or eight goats from the rock cliffs by the sea in Alaska.

After Uncle Jim had been in Alaska for a while and things didn't go so great in the romance department, he decided to go home to Scotland and woo his high school sweetheart from Harthill and bring her to America. That's exactly what he did; went home, got Helen Tobin O'Donnell who was originally from Dublin made her Helen T. McCleary and brought her to the United States - Alaska. Jim and Helen McCleary had six kids in rapid-fire succession: Eileen, Colleen, Maureen, James, Robert Hunter, and Patrick. Jim's wife Helen was a wonderful singer and people enjoyed her singing very much. Jim was in Alaska a total of ten years and then they relocated to Portland, Oregon, 200 miles from Richland along the Columbia Gorge. Uncle Jim was a longshoreman in Portland on the docks along the Columbia River upstream from Astoria where the river joins the Pacific Ocean.

When my dad and Uncle Howard were in their latter teens they got jobs in Richland working at Lee's Tahitian, a Chinese-American (funnily called Tahitian) restaurant and bar in the Uptown Shopping Center. The Uptown was the hub of social activity in Richland. It's a big square, couple of city block sized complex of stores and restaurants hooked together. It still stands today and some of the original merchants are still there: Spudnut Donuts made with potato flour (ran by Italian family), the Uptown Tavern and Lee's Tahitian. In the big square mall were BB&M Sporting Goods, Hurt's clothing for women, Dawson Richards clothing for men, Parker Hardware, Newberry's dime store and lunch counter. The Uptown movie theater with its tall neon sign with an atom on top sat on the corner of the low slung mid-century style mall. Over time more shops moved in and the Uptown was booming as was all of post WWII/Cold War era Richland. Johnny's Delicatessen was in the Uptown, Lerner's and A&Z Clothing, the Elite Shop, Lancaster's, Tom McCann shoes. Down the street was Tim's Drive in with the great ham and cheese po'boy and Bye's Burgers where Aunt Dona worked.

Uncle Howard and my dad were dishwashers and worked in the kitchen of Lee's Tahitian Chinese Restaurant and one fateful day were sitting behind in the alleyway peeling potatoes into a bucket between them. Along strolled Susie Fisher, who was the spunky, pretty blond that Uncle Howard was going with at the time. With her was a dark haired, brown-eyed demure beauty that Jack had never seen before. He said to Howard, "Who's that girl with Susie Fisher?" Howie said, "Oh that's Linda Rawlings, her best friend." Dad said that mom saw him and "liked the cut of him" so he pursued her, even though he was four years older. He eventually won her over with his wit and charm and Sunny Jim good looks. So they double dated a lot, my dad and my mom along with Uncle Howard and Susie Fisher. Sue Fisher is still mom's best friend to this day, since the 3rd grade, around 60 years.

My mother Linda Rawlings, was the anti-Jack, a very shy and sheltered only child from New York, and was pretty overwhelmed with the wild, outgoing and competitive McClearys when she started going with my dad. The sheer number of the people in the family and the intensity level were a shock to her since she was from a family of three, total. Eventually my mom got used to it and could hold her own quite well, became a force in her own right. On the other side of the romance it took my dad longer to win over my super-conservative English and Swedish grandfather from western New York, Bud Rawlings. To my mom's dad, Jack appeared to be a greaser, a hoodlum and from the wrong part of town and not what he had in mind at all for his only child. My maternal grandma Mary "Jane" Rawlings, who was kind of a wildcat herself liked Jack right away. She even stood beside him in a couple of scuffles with neighbors in later years and put in her 2 cents worth of smart ass comments to back Jack up. It was an uphill battle at first with Bud but in a short time my dad's charm, politeness and sincerity about wanting to spend time with their dark eyed daughter won Bud over. Jack and Bud became very close and when my grandparents died in the mid-1990s their son-in-law had been their best friend for years.

My mom and dad drove down to Tastee Freeze Drive-in in Richland in the 52 Ford that my dad had: his brothers all did their courtin' in the old 48 Ford. They each got a burger and a pop and parked down the hill from Columbia High School, Home of the Bombers, where my mom had just graduated and Jack four years before. They had dated for quite a while and while they were very different they enjoyed each other's company immensely. My dad could always make my reserved mother laugh, even to the point of tears – and when my mom laughs really hard she looks like my grandma Jane Rawlings. Sitting in the car by the football stadium they decided to get married. It was 1963, they got married that September. My oldest brother Jon Andrew was born in December of 1964.

My dad went to the local junior college and got degree in drafting and engineering when he and my mom first married. At the same time he had a job working for the City of Richland as a janitor, then he moved up to the Parks and Recreation Department and mowed parks and did maintenance work around Richland. These city jobs were good, stable jobs to have. I was born in October of 1966. On the day that I was born he said to my mom, "You got your little girl."

Jack's big career break came when he got a position drafting for the Richland Water Department and had finally arrived, with his own office and briefcase and name plate on the desk. One day my mom came to see him at the office with me, age one, and Jon, three, in tow and told my dad that she was pregnant with twins. Michael James and Joseph LeRoy were born October 1968 at Kadlec Hospital in Richland. My three siblings and I were born at Kadlec Hospital, named for a Hanford project engineer, Lt. Col Harry R. Kadlec, that apparently died of overwork and was the first fatality in the new hospital.

Jack McCleary was ambitious and wanted to pay his own way, not owe anyone money, so he tested and became Richland Firefighter. Jack and Linda owned their government issue Ranch house on Cottonwood Drive and got down to raising us kids. My dad worked 24 hour shifts at the fire house so he was away a lot and my mom took care of the four of us - all four years old and under. Always trying to move his family ahead my dad was a door to door wig and hairpiece salesman for a time. He liked a good get-rich-quick scheme, but after schlepping Miss Dianna's Wigs around on his days off as part of their "Independent Broker Program," he realized it wasn't the vehicle he was looking for.

My mother always thought that Jack's sister Bev, former Miss Richland, was the coolest, most glamorous person around and loved to spend time with her. Since she was a fairly new mom with all these little ones, my other aunt, Dona, took Linda under her wing and taught her what she knew about being a mother and an organized housekeeper. My mother became really close with my Grandma Jean and spent lots of time with her on Ranch Road with us kids. They would sit and visit all day drinking black tea with canned Carnation milk in it and Grandma Jean smoking the Tarytons like a house-afire. They chatted and watched Grandma Jean's soap operas, The Guiding Light and One Life to Live, all day, with the twins in the playpen and Jon and me running around the place. When it was about 30 minutes until Pawn was due home from the Hanford Area and my dad due to come over from the Firehouse, they'd jump up and get busy. Grandma Jean would pan fry chicken breasts and boil potatoes and Linda would race around with the Bissell sweeper cleaning the carpet. The accelerated cooking steamed up all the windows in the front of the small house and they'd laugh while they worked to be ready for the husbands to get home.

Grandma Jean had a distinctive Old Country brogue, more so than Pawn, and had a rhyme that she'd say to all the babies and grandbabies in the family and that my dad always said too. It went: "Roon a boot, Roon a boot, catch a wee mouse…" as you make circles on the child's palm with your forefinger. "Up he goes, up he goes" climbing up the arm, "in the wee house!" tickle under the armpit. Baby goes crazy laughing. I've heard this rhyme all my life and saw my dad do it with all his grandkids. I'm in my 40s and just realized that Grandma Jean was saying "round about" but it sounded like "roon a boot" with the Old Country accent.

At the Desert Inn, the mini Sands Hotel of Washington, Jean McCleary continued her reign as the most respected queen bee of the place. Grandma Jean was the banquet manager and ran that part of the business for years. My aunts, Anna and Dona both worked there under the tutelage of the master and learned a lot about service; Uncle Howard got a job in the Desert Inn cooking and over time worked up to chef. Grandma Jean was always decked out in her black and white waitress uniform, in the summer sometimes it was a pink and white uniform. She always had on makeup and lipstick. When her daughters worked there, Grandma Jean would send them running around getting food prepped and ready in the kitchen and loading their trays to serve at the banquet. As soon as they trays were perfect and they were at the door, Grandma Jean would take their tray and walk in with a flourish and a smile to serve the important guests. The glory went to mother.

On September 23, 1963, Jean served the most prestigious diner of her career. JFK. President John F. Kennedy came to Hanford to the dedication of the N Reactor and talked about the Nuclear Test Ban Treaty to the crowd gathered. President Kennedy arrived in a helicopter and touched down on the Hanford site to deliver a rousing speech. A limited number of people could attend the speech, security was tight - so mainly Hanford workers were there, but they numbered in the thousands. After the speech the Presidential entourage came to the Desert Inn and my Grandma Jean managed and served the luncheon banquet for the President. I guarantee on the day the President came for lunch, Grandma Jean carried the tray to the head table in the banquet. Just two months later in Dallas he was assassinated while in his motorcade with Mrs. Kennedy. Grandma Jean had an interesting career in the service business: Henry Ford, Ann Cody – Buffalo Bill's sister, Oppenheimer, JFK, not bad for a farm girl from Slemish Mountain, Northern Ireland.

Richland in the Cold War years after WWII was still a boomtown as it had been in the 1940s. Eventually, a total of nine nuclear reactors were built on the 550 acre desert site alongside the river. There was ample work with plutonium extracting and refinishing, research laboratories, a nuclear power plant and other research projects. Richland was the kind of place where you could climb out of a menial job and right into a really good job on the Site if you had your wits about you. For example, the old friends the Watts: Mrs. Watts worked at the café with Jean for years then got a job on site in the laundry and then was bumped up to a nuclear technician, her husband Earl Watts, was in the Carpenters with Pawn and ended up a respected engineer, some say a genius, on the Hanford site with a bunch of patents in his name once his talents were recognized. My Uncle Larry, who married Aunt Dona and cooked with Uncle Howard in the Desert Inn kitchen, met some influential people at the Desert Inn and trained as a radiation technician and did that work until his retirement, decades later. Uncle Larry was also the sole caretaker of Harold McClusky, the man that was irradiated in 1976 at the Hanford site[38] with the highest dose of radiation by any living human. Uncle Larry was the only one allowed to go near "The Atomic Man" wearing full hazmat gear to test his radiation levels. My Uncle Charlie, who married Aunt Bev, worked for the research laboratory where they did testing on beagles to see the effect of smoke on animals, what were called the smoking beagles. Charlie was the caretaker of the animals. There was so much work in Richland that if you were a warm body with the capacity to learn and some ambition you could have a great career.

Local legend has always said Richland has more PhDs per capita than any city in the US. I've worked on the Hanford site writing and editing documents regarding the cleanup of the nuclear waste in the government's effort to restore the land to safety. My brother is a Union craftsman at Hanford and his team recently demolished Kadlec, the hospital that my siblings and I were born in. At some point the hospital was uprooted from its place in downtown Richland and taken to the Hanford site, where it sat until it was decimated the other day. Our grandpas built Hanford; we are cleaning up Hanford. On the Hanford site you will meet many locals that are the third generation Hanford workers with a story similar to mine.

When we were kids and Pawn was in the Carpenters Union working at Hanford he bent 60 penny (long and heavy) nails in half for our entertainment while we sat around his chair in awe. These nails were so big they looked like railroad spikes to us. Pawn, my dad and Uncle Howard would all compete on the chin up (what some call pull up) bar too. In those days, the 1970s, Pawn was an old man, yet performed these tricks of toughness and competed with his boys. He could still do the one armed pullups. Pawn also did chinups at age 70 with his grandson Tod holding on around his neck and hanging on his back. My grandpa roofed his last house at age 73. The old man (which is what his sons and grandsons called him) though thin was a tougher than wang leather. (Jack saying, I have no idea what it means.)

Some of the McClearys - especially my dad and grandpa Pawn - could debate someone into submission too. Many in the family are very smart, both street and book, and could talk someone into a corner pretty quickly. Pawn loved to have the traveling Mormon or Jehovah's Witness missionaries knock on his door. He'd invite them in for a cup of tea and a conversation about theology. These talks were civil and non-confrontational, even friendly; he was curious about various religions and about people.

Pawn, a predictable man of routine, ate a cheese sandwich, open faced and a jam sandwich the same way quite often with a cup of tea. Two cheese, one jam. This is what the miners brought to work in their piece boxes back in Scotland. You can take the man out of the mine, but you can't take mining out of the man. And you didn't sit in his swivel rocking chair when he came with his food. My cousin Scott did once and got thrown out the front door, literally, by Pawn. "Christ man, what's wrong with you?"

Uncle Jim, who had finally acclimated to American life, and his wife Helen and kids – Eileen, Colleen, Maureen, Patrick, James and Robert-came from Portland Oregon to visit on Ranch Road fairly often. They were a sight to behold, rolling up in a big, old, dusty car with their clothes in the trunk, loose. When it was time to dress in clean clothes the next day the kids went out, popped the trunk and grabbed something to wear. My Uncle Tony came out for these visits and played the guitar for the family's entertainment. Uncle Tony married and had a son Robert (Bobby) McCleary, a talented guitarist himself that goes by the name Duncan Pryce. Life was good on Ranch Road in West Richland in the 1960s and 70s.

In Richland proper, my dad had established himself as the storyteller and one of the jokesters of the firehouse. The man could tell a story and loved an audience. He had stories about hunting, growing up in Richland, playing pool and people that he knew, with impressions. My dad saw the absurd in life and loved to poke fun at it. He loved to make people laugh. Jack never cussed around women much, but I guess among the men he was quite hard core with the swearing and blue stories. The men worked consecutive 24 hour shifts and had little bedrooms there, so they were together a lot. The guys took turns cooking for the rest of the crew and my dad made a mean green pepper steak with red wine served over rice. Danny Downs was the fried chicken king of the department and taught my dad to make delicious chicken.

Along with fighting fires, my dad was a paramedic and ambulance driver for the City of Richland. The battalion chief, he called "batt chief" was Red McCulley during my dad's tenure with the department. My mom and we kids visited my dad a lot at the firehouse that sat right beside the Columbia River. There was a dike between the two and my brothers and I rolled down the slope on our sides, the freshly cut green grass cushioning us on the way down. Afterward, you'd itch like mad from the grass but it was worth it, the slope of that dike seemed endless. Inside the firehouse we were told to watch out for the fire trucks and only walk through along the wall behind the massive red trucks and white ambulance. There was a tower for drying the hoses out after a fire and metal stairs going up about three floors amongst the hoses. The wet fabric on the outside of the water hoses gave the stairwell a damp musty odor and the way the long hoses hooked three floors up hung down it was a jungle of damp fingers of fabric. We loved to run up and down the stairs in the tower. My dad responded to many fires and accidents in homes and on the road and the trauma of seeing so many hurt and suffering people affected him a great deal. He didn't have the stomach for really sad things.

Out at the family property, Pawn was old school with his home remedies and didn't believe in doctors --or lawyers for that matter. He called them 'parasites', and said they were feeding off the misery of others. My cousin Tod lived with his mom in the apartment that Pawn had tacked onto the back of his house until he was about seven and was Pawn's right hand man. He's the one that would hold Pawn's neck and hang down his back while he did the chin-ups. When Tod got sick with a cold Pawn would break out the mold that he collected from the ever-present sharp cheddar cheese on the table under the dome and force him to eat it. Similarly, when Tod had an ear-ache as a little kid, Pawn warmed up some vinegar, held Tod down on the kitchen floor and poured it into his ailing ear. Tod said that was the last earache he ever had. Or maybe the last he ever admitted to for fear of having another treatment. Pawn would break out his 40 year old pocket knife, and lift a foreign object out of your eye with it if you had something stuck in it. Pretty soon, you'd not mention that you had something in your eye even if it was the size of the Washington Monument. Getting out slivers with the same dirty, germy knife was not fun either. Howie says his dad would dig in like coring an apple, or go in under and flap the skin up, and that they probably should have had stitches after a sliver removal.

As much as Pawn was hard on the boys in general and hard on the whole family with the medical procedures, he also didn't let anyone mess with his children. On Ranch Road there wasn't a lot of fruit or vegetables to eat and Howard and Jack and their friends would go steal from gardens to eat on the spot or bring home whatever was in season. Once they were stealing grapes from the farmer, Old "Stonewall" Jackson, and he threw golf ball sized cement balls at the boys' backs while they were hunched over picking. They came and showed Pawn the welts and out the door he went. Howie says he grabbed Old Stonewall by the shirt collar and said, "What do you think you are doing, you chicken shit son of a bitch."

On Ranch Road, my grandparents gave one acre of land to all of their eight children to build a house on. Pawn lived the credo "share and share alike" and doling out of the exact same amount of land to all the kids pleased him very much. In Ireland, it was a tradition in old times to give each son (legitimate and illegitimate) equal parts of the farm when the father died. Later in poor times, the farms went to the eldest son only or one of the selected legitimate sons. In America, Pawn and Jean kept the older tradition alive and of course included their girls. All of them: Bev, Betty, Anna, Dona, Jack, Howard, Jim and Tony, were given a vacant one-acre lot on which to build a house. All the lots were joined in a big block and this became what I call the McCleary compound, our own little Hyannis Port, minus the Cape Cod frontage. Pawn and Grandma Jean's workshop turned house was the anchor on the corner.

When Jack got his piece of the world from his parents he started planning. Our family of six was living in Richland on Cottonwood Dr. in the Ranch house that my parents bought and remodeled. They had just heard about some ready-made houses for sale. All you had to do was choose a house and have it moved to your land. The catch was the houses were on a defunct military base in Moses Lake about 75 miles north along the Columbia River from West Richland. My parents, very excited - mom was always game for adventure especially about houses and design, drove up to walk around the abandoned base with its barracks, empty houses and vacant military buildings and chose a house. They were not big, very dirty and in rough shape but they found one they liked and paid for it. Then a semi-truck moved the house, in one piece - dirt, bugs, mice and all - to W. Richland. It was rolled in and placed on the lot right next to my grandparents' house on the corner of Ranch Road and 46th. Our house needed more rooms so my Dad, with some help from Pawn and Bud, extended the house on both ends. Our house had French windows and other unusual details that my parents picked out together. No money was saved by rolling in the house from the military base, as opposed to building it from scratch, but dad was always a bit eccentric.

Aunt Bev and Uncle Charlie, the champion lunch box holder, built their house on the lot south of ours. Their home was a modern rambler style house and my older teenage cousins, three of them, lived there so the place always had an air of coolness to me. My Aunt Bev got more beautiful as the years went by and it was so fun to be on Ranch Road with the family. Uncle Howard, his wife Barbara and daughter Lori built their nice brown house on the 46th street side of the property, soon after Aunt Betty (Bumps) and her husband Bill came from the grocery business in California and made a home on their land next to Uncle Howard's place.

Uncle Howard smoked Camels, no filter (still does, actually) and when he ran out living on Ranch Road, he'd write a note stating his name, that he was an adult and his desire for a pack of smokes and sent it and cash with us kids and we'd walk up to the Foodliner. Howie gave us extra money to buy candy for our trouble. It was about a mile walk up the gravel hill onto the pavement and down to the store; my brothers and I liked the adventure of going for cigs. West Richland in the summer was always hot and dry, on the gravel road there was powder dust flying around your legs as you walked. The Russian olive trees that grew where there was a little moisture in a pond or stream smelled acidy and strong like sage. You had to watch out for rattlesnakes, which were spotted pretty regularly around the town and the desert beyond. Behind the small grocery store was Flat Top, a big desert mountain about 800 ft. high. There was a switch-backing path to the top and you could climb up its bald face, with the acrid smelling sagebrush here and there and see out across West Richland with the Yakima River snaking through. We hiked up there in our dusty Converse once in a while and on the top of the mountain stood a huge metal cross, about 16 feet high (or it seemed to seven year old me) and painted white. Standing beside this big cross on the flat top of a desert mountain I knew this was part of the "Religious Bullshit" that I heard my dad and Pawn talking about.

Our grandpa Pawn would drive me, my three brothers and the odd cousin in the big turquoise with white leather Mercury Marauder up to the Double AA or the A and A he called it, to get some candy -- the force of gravity pinning us to the back seat as we went up the big gravel hill to town. Of course we were standing on the back seat, no seat belt or, God forbid, car-seats in those days. My mom watched in horror, but you didn't cross the old man. Yes, Pawn's driving was fast and reckless from what I can remember and all part of the Pawn mystique. He also pronounced my name, Suzy, with a Scottish brogue like, "Suuessssssy," really drawn out and cool.

What I remember about my immigrant grandparents are the lemon drops, the sharp cheddar cheese sandwiches, the milky tea in old china cups – and the smoking, good God the smoking. When we would visit on Ranch Road, Pawn had a ritual of going to the white metal kitchen cupboard and getting out the bag of lemon drops. There were a couple of green lemon drops in the bag of mostly yellow ones and he said the green ones were lucky. We grandkids, all wanted green. If you got a green, you felt like a superstar. Pawn always said, "One per customer" in his funny way of talking while holding out the crackly cellophane candy bag. My mom says he passed out the small hard candies to all the grandkids, regardless of age or eating ability. The lemon shaped drops were the perfect size to lodge in the throat of a toddler, so my mom scrambled to get the candy from us and break off some small pieces while the old man wasn't looking.

At my grandparents' house, I would sit on the itchy, thin wool carpet in front of the big TV with the spindly legs and watch Perry Mason. Those shows always ended the same with someone exclaiming from the courtroom gallery, "I did it!" Grandma Jean liked to watch basketball games on TV and hardly ever missed a game. My brothers and I would go to the grandparents' house on New Year 's Eve babysat by one of the older cousins while all the grownups were having a party at an aunt or uncle's house. Probably that blasted Hogmaney ritual. We listened to the top 100 songs of the year on the radio while we waited for the New Year to come along and our parents to come back and get us. We'd just walk out the door and across the field to our house next door. It was a simple way to live amongst family.

Oh, The Aunts: there are four of them. They always appeared in a pack to the baby showers, Tupperware parties, family weddings, McCleary family Christmas parties, picnics at the river - shoulder to shoulder, gifts in hand, good looking and stylish ladies, all with some form of the McCleary look. All four came to all family events and sat in straight backed chairs in a row, a panel of women, my dad's older sisters. The Aunts are Beverley, Anna, Dona and Betty (nicknamed Bumps). I always thought Betty was called Bumps for her impressive boobs, but it turns out, no – at the 4 Mile in Butte there were three little girls named Betty in the 1930s so our Betty was called Betty Bumps, later shortened to just Bumps. I've always called this committee of women The Aunts. My dad's four older sisters: a force of nature- a force to be reckoned with, lined up in the old family photos in pencil skirts, spiky, pointy 60s pumps, with their sexy best leg forward and bouffants up to the sky.

106

Grandma Jean loved to order from mail order catalogs and had a penchant for these 1960s tabletop light contraptions. They had plastic spines cascading out of a base, and you flipped a switch and it glowed with all sorts of colors all over the room. Very fancy, I thought. And grandma liked to order Christmas treats and get them in the mail. When Pawn and Jean went home to Ireland and Scotland a few times they brought back souvenirs for the family including my other grandparents, the Rawlings. I have many of these items today: sewing kit in a plaid case, a tartan plaid wool tam, linen handkerchiefs in a box from Ireland. I've inherited a portrait of Pawn's brother Robert in the Royal Air Force in Scotland. Pawn always said that this brother borrowed $1500 from him in 1960 then disappeared and ended up selling typewriters in England. So Pawn "wrote him off" and never talked to him again.

We liked living in West Richland, my dad called "West" and our house imported from the defunct Army camp was transformed by my dad into a very nice home. We had a wood burning stove inside and it was kind of hippie in décor. It sat up on a knoll that dad had built up before the house arrived because of the threat of floods that could come when the Yakima River got high and broke out of its banks. My dad didn't like to owe anyone money and loved acquiring things for the family. Case in point: next to the Jack McCleary one acre of land, not on Pawn's side but the other side, was some more acreage owned by an old hermit named Abe. This land was covered, and I mean covered with junk and Abe lived in a little hovel in the middle of old cars and wood piles and farm equipment and just plain garbage. My dad befriended Abe; he never cared about anyone's station in life. The more of an underdog you were, the more he liked you. Abe agreed to sell my dad his land adjoining ours and move out. Crazy thing was my dad bought the junkyard too. He didn't have Abe clear out the 50 years of trash and junk, he took possession of that too. So old Abe took the money and ran. Let me assure you it was really hard, dirty work clearing out Abe's house/shed and the land. I've suffered from a lifetime phobia of mice because of that experience.

Fighting Fires and Neighbors

In the early years of all of us McClearys living on the property amongst each other things were good. Then some outsiders bought some of our property and moved in. That's when the wheels came off and fighting commenced with my dad, my uncle, and Pawn against the new neighbor. There were several big donnybrooks and guns drawn on both sides. My dad had a spectacular fist fight on the gravel road with the patriarch of the outsiders. Wearing his City of Richland fireman uniform, my dad and his nemesis fought their way off the road and into the ditch. The grand finale was when the neighbor came over in the dark of night, on Christmas Eve, and blasted the windshield out of my uncle's two cars with a shotgun. Of course that made the paper, with my grandpa lounging across the hood of the decimated front of the car showing off the destruction. This large photo and story was front page news. In the text of the article the Sheriff says that it was a Hatfield and McCoy feud and the McClearys and their rivals better cool it before someone got killed. The reporter mentions that the deputies had been called out to the property three times in as many months. It was pointed out in the article that James "Scotty" McCleary and his family were immigrants from Scotland. Let me say though, that was **40 years** earlier and he'd been a US citizen for 30 years, but the reporter mentioned it anyway: maybe it explained the explosive behavior. The outsiders had moved in from California. No comment on their breeding and pedigree. My dad and the neighbor would yell and cuss over the fence, turn off each other's water, cut fences and never did resolve the dispute. Fighting: a family tradition. Outsiders moving in: the undoing of the rural McCleary compound.

We had farm animals on Ranch Road and we'd go to the livestock sale in Prosser and Sunnyside, two small towns up the Yakima Valley, with our dad to buy animals. Dad called it The Sale and when he got in the old Ford truck and said let's go to The Sale, we'd jump right in. Over time, we bought lambs and sheep, pigs and piglets, a goat and a horse. We kept some of them as pets, like an aggressive and angry sheep that we named Bucky. He was a bucker if you tried to sit on his back and liked to haul off and ram people with his rock hard skull. We bought another sheep at the sale that we named Sally and she was the last left unpurchased at the end of the day because she had a huge watermelon-like tumor on her side back near her butt. No one would buy the deformed older sheep, so we did. Sally was a pet on our makeshift farm and we loved her. Much to my mom's annoyance, Jack would take us to The Sale to buy new animals and then figure out the pens and fencing when he got home.

My three brothers and I liked to ride the sheep out in the pasture. When you were four or five years old riding a full grown sheep is pretty thrilling. The wool on a sheep is really rough, like a Brillo pad and my little pale legs got scratched up riding in a short dress and dusty Converse sneakers. With BB and pellet guns that we had around the place, my brothers and I, and our friends, waged battles shooting sheep poop at each other through the guns. We really weren't supposed to be riding the sheep, but we did it anyway and my dad would yell from the house to the pasture,

"Get off those sheep, you're GONNA bust your ass!" The man never said, take care, or be careful, or watch yourself, it was always "DON'T bust your ass!"

My dad worked at the Richland firehouse while my mom was home wrangling us kids and the animals. One day the fencing failed again when my dad was working and all the pigs and piglets got loose. My dad and Howard bought 20 piglets and were slopping them with the food scraps from my uncle's cooking job at Hills on the Mall. My mom tried to herd the pigs back to the pen; the pen for the 20 was at our house. My mom, though pretty strong and athletic from hard work, couldn't get them so she called Uncle Howie at the restaurant, screeching for him to get home and help her. My dad couldn't leave the firehouse. Howard showed up post haste, billowing powder dust behind his car. He chased all the swine up the hill on Ranch Road that dropped sharply down to our houses. A grown man in his chef whites and black work shoes chasing a bunch of pigs up the gravel road in 100 degree summer swelter. Eventually he got 19 of them and herded them home. And said the hell with the last one since he was about to die from the heat. He chalked that one up as a casualty in the life of new pig farmers.

Two or three nights later Howie was coming home from the restaurant in the dark and as he left the pavement and hit the gravel and started down the hill to his house he saw something in his headlights. The ass of a little piglet wiggling along as it ran down the hill. Howard couldn't believe it, it was that damned 20th pig. He drove slowly behind it and watched it scramble down the hill and off in the direction of the pig pen. After parking, he went and took a head count in the pen and it was back in with the rest. Howard says pigs are one of the smartest animals, along with dolphins, that cows and goats are dumb as hell but pigs are smart. #20 was pretty smart.

One day Pawn was about to cut his grass and looked through the barbed wire fence and saw our flock of sheep out in the field between his house and ours. He had an idea: the sheep could mow his lawn for him. He had my dad bring them over to graze their way around his yard and went inside to have a smoke and a cup of tea. A while later he came out to see how they were doing. "Jaaaeeezus Christ Almighty!!... those sheep are shitting everywhere, get them out of here!" Pawn shouted over to my dad. The mowing master plan was a dismal failure.

Pawn was a barber for all the grandsons and he'd drag a chrome stool with steps on the front out to the back patio. An extension cord was strung from his workshop in the garage out to the patio and the clippers were plugged in and fired up. All the boys: the 3 Chickenitos, my brother Jon, cousins Gregg and Troy and any others around all had a turn on the stool to get their hair buzzed by Pawn after he wrapped a towel around their shoulders to keep the hair off. My mom was really fussy about her kids' haircuts and Pawn's hairstyles were a nightmare. You just got what you got. My mom said that this, the possibility of your baby choking on a lemon drop and Pawn blasting up the hill in the Mercury and later the LTD with us kids standing on the back seat, vulnerable little heads visible in the back window, were the things that made her nervous about her father-in-law.

My dad and Uncle Howard liked to have a drink once in a while; especially Howard. There was a bar in Kennewick, the next town over, called the Hayloft and one night my dad and Howie went to have a beer and shoot pool. The bartender, Rocky, was a recent transplant from New York City and thought Jack and Howard looked like a couple of country saps. It was a slow night at the tavern and Rocky challenged them to a pool game. So they started to play, Jack or Howard against Rocky. They won every game but Rocky refused to quit; he thought eventually he would beat these young small town Irish punks. By the time the smoke cleared, they had played at least 40 games total and both had a wad of money that rolled up to about three inches thick. Rocky was pissed off and glad to see them go. When the Tri-City Herald came out the next day, there was a banner on the front page that said "Hayloft Bartender skips town absconding with the Tavern's till money." It actually ended up in the pockets of Jack and Howard McCleary.

Uncle Howard became notorious in Richland for fighting and raising hell and was in trouble or hurt much of the time. This was the case from when he was small all the way up to the 1990s when he was in his 60s and finally started to tone it down. The Benton County Sherriff's Office and Richland Police Department breathed a collective sigh of relief. Howie told me that he did about half of the stuff that people in Richland said he did, the other half he didn't. Uncle Howard estimates himself that he's been in 600 fights in his life and lost about half of them and his arrests for alcohol related offenses are mighty high too. He's now 69 and put the bottle down for good some years back.

Pawn finished his shift on the Hanford site where he enjoyed a good reputation and was proud of the quality carpenter work he had done there for decades as a Union man. He jumped in and lit a cig then headed home in his Special Edition 1962-1963 Marauder to Ranch Road. Grandma Jean finished her shift as banquet manager at the Desert Inn, sat on her car seat with her legs out the open door of her metallic burnt orange- red Mercury Turnpike Cruiser, slipped out of her sensible work shoes and put on her signature metallic flats that were folded in half in a little bag, then headed home herself. Both cars came smoking with powder dust out of their ass ends down the gravel hill on 46th Ave. to their house, one behind the other, parking in front of the modest, but still respectable house with the pitched roof. Jean and Jim stood together, her in black and white waitress dress with a rhinestone brooch on the collar and him in his white carpenter overalls and white t-shirt, in the yard that was hard to care for with cheat grass and crab grass choking out the little bit of real grass, and looked across at what they had.

Land: they had a piece of America for themselves and all their children, all together – share and share alike, one per customer. It's what they wanted when they left the Old Country, though they didn't know then what it would look like and how they would get there. They sent for their son Jim and he had finally made it to America. The James McCleary family was all together and had security purchased entirely with their hard work. Their kids were happy and successful, for the most part: a firefighter, business women and men, a chef, excellent mothers. Not one coal miner or domestic servant in the bunch. Jim and Jean, the Irish immigrants who, in their early 20s, separately boarded ships from Scotland and crossed the Atlantic Ocean for ten days to a life they could not imagine, were home.

In 1971, when my dad was a Richland firefighter, paramedic and ambulance driver, all the family, including my mother and brothers, were on Ranch Road for an April Fool's Day yard clean up at Pawn and Grandma Jeans house. My dad was on duty that day and his beloved mother, Grandma Jean collapsed at the house on Ranch Road after a surgery on her leg veins. Howard says she leaned up to him on the couch and said, "Do you have a match son?" then just kept on going down to the floor. The call came into the Richland Firehouse and they, including my dad, came out to my grandparent's house on Ranch Road. All the cousins were herded onto the back patio in hushed tones and I knew something was very wrong. I was five years old. My dad tried to save his mom in the house and in the ambulance on the way to the hospital but did not. Grandma Jean died on April 1st, 1971 at age 66 from an aneurysm in her leg. It was a heartbreak that he carried with him always: not being able to save his mother.

In 1973, I was a shy, fair, freckly second-generation Irish American kindergartener at the Hanford School. It was an experimental school and all the Hanford worker offspring attended one school for kindergarten through 12th grade. My teacher was Mrs. Padgett and part of her class was the "show & tell"; kids brought in all kind of special relics to show. I brought new baby lambs to school. The lambs, three of them, were loaded into the truck and brought to school by my mom and dad. I wore a short 70s jumper, plaid (my mom dressed me in plaid for important occasions), with my bare white legs, holding court with my farm animals on a little island of hay in the Kindergarten classroom. Lambs are not soft and fluffy like you would think from cartoons and books, the wooly hair is coarse and lambs are hard to pet. Your hand doesn't glide along it gets hung up in the rough fur. New lambs are not small either, they are gangly and strong. The local newspaper came out and took photos of me and my classmates with the lambs. Posing with the headstrong animals was not easy. The next day, I was on the front page of the Tri-City Herald with a write-up inspired by "Mary had a little Lamb." My dad took time off from the firehouse to make my spectacular show and tell happen. My Rawlings grandmother bought 30 papers; there are still copies of my face and the lamb's face floating around in old scrapbooks, photo albums and suitcases - even decoupaged on wooden plaques to hang on the wall. Newspaper cover 1970s: my first moment of greatness.

The Flood

In 1974, the Yakima River swelled above its banks and crept out onto the flood plain at Ranch Road. It didn't flood very often, no one could remember the last time. The year it flooded was both exciting and terrifying for me as a six year old child. We could see the water from the river, which was usually not even visible from Ranch Road, slowly coming toward us. We had reports coming in on the big, turquoise rotary dial phone that Uncle Howard's was getting close to having water inside, Aunt Bev's house the same. Pawn's house was taking on water.

The dirty water was rising slowly but steadily and we brought all the animals, sheep and lambs, out of the pens and up on higher ground around the house. It was kind of a Noah's Ark situation. Our canoe and small rowboat were pulled up onto dry land too. I started to get worried; we were surrounded by dirty dishwater with tumbleweeds floating in it. Always calm in an emergency from riding the ambulance, my dad realized at a

112

certain point that we needed to evacuate. The water was trapping us up in our house. I didn't want the water to come in and ruin the house that my dad had just built, and our new shag wall to wall carpeting, and the wallpaper that my mother had just hung that looked like old newsprint, and the turquoise linoleum on the kitchen floor!

My dad and my un-girly, scrappy mother loaded us in the canoe and the boat two kids in each and paddled up Ranch Road, past the junkyard, further and further to the base of the hill at Ranch Road, a distance of about ¼ mile. It was hard work paddling through the murky water with weeds floating randomly through it and the odd plastic child's toy from one of the houses. Soon us kids were safely out of the middle of the flooding, and there was water covering all the land and inching up into old barns in the distance. My other grandparents, the Rawlings, were up on the top of the hill waiting to get the four of us, wrap us up in blankets and take us in to their house in Richland. My mom and dad went back in the boats and started to bring the sheep and dogs and other animals out. Luckily we didn't have a horse at that time. Balancing a frightened sheep or two in a canoe wasn't easy. My dad paddled and mom wrangled the animals.

Pawn and Grandma Jean's house sat much lower and got a lot of water inside, enough to damage everything in the house and imbue the place with a musty odor that never went away. Uncle Howard, and his family, and Aunt Bev, and her family, evacuated in a fishing boat driven by a drunk family friend. Aunt Betty and Uncle Bill managed to get out too and their house, along with all the other houses, was left empty and abandoned in a deep sea of muddy water. A guy floated by hanging onto a log and managed to get up into Betty's house, put on some dry clothes of Uncle Bills, and eat some food. He waited out the flood in their house, strangers to him.

The flood waters were pretty calm at our house on the Ranch Road side of the McCleary compound, but the Yakima River had diverted through the 46th Ave. side. Uncle Howard says it was like the Colorado River outside his door. He had a wood pile about five feet tall sitting by his house and had placed a car battery atop the wood pile some time before the flood. During the height of the flooding the wood pile was picked up by the water and moved to the corner of his yard against the fence some 40 yards away. The car battery still on top. So in the flood of 74, we avoided getting water into our house, as did Howard, Beverley and Betty, but it decimated everything around us. Pawn's house got the worst of it since it sat at a lower elevation.

Ranch Road in the summer (it seemed like it was always summer there) was hot, dusty and dry, but around the marshy banks of the Yakima river nearby the mosquitoes bred like mad and then came over to visit. Everyone was terrorized by the mosquitos in West Richland and in the town of Richland. The mosquito truck drove down into the McCleary estate at the junction of Ranch Road and 46th Ave. on hot summer evenings and sprayed the mosquito spray out of a huge tank on its bed. We ran along behind it in the clouds of mist having a grand old time frolicking in the poison.

Jack McCleary,
(left) 1949

Jack,(l) Jim,
Howie, back row
below.
Dona,(l) Betty,
Anna, Beverley(r)
below.
1950, when Jim
came from
Scotland.

Beverley
McCleary and
Kirk Douglas,
Desert Inn
Richland, WA

Bev at U.S.
Savings Bonds
ceremony,
Richland
(all 1950)

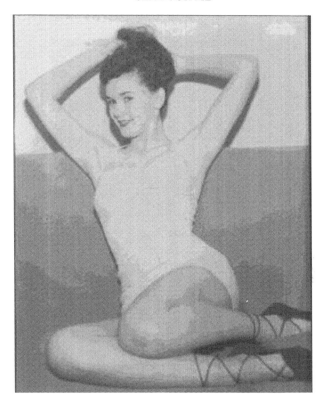

Bev, 1950 modeling and Miss Richland parade

Jack (l) & Howie McCleary @ Rawlings house on Dallas St. Richland 1961. Below: author's mother Linda Rawlings 1962, High School graduation.

Above: Jane Rawlings (l), James and Jean McCleary 1966. Lower: James "Pawn" McCleary (l) & Jack McCleary 1970. Note: arms folded.

Anna(l), Linda Rawlings McCleary, Beverley & Dona McCleary (r)
Below: Uncle Jim McCleary (l), Pawn, Jack, Bud Rawlings, Linda
& Jon McCleary, Grandma Jean, Jane Rawlings, Tod Williams (r)

James "Pawn"
McCleary 25th
anniversary on
the Hanford Site.

Suzanne
McCleary from
Tri-City Herald,
Hanford School
1973

CHAPTER 11

KENNEWICK, WASHINGTON - 1974

A while after all hell broke loose with the neighbor on Ranch Road, my parents bought a beautiful, but dilapidated farm in rural east Kennewick and we flew the coop. The house was a two story classic-style farmhouse with four screened-in wrap-around porches, built in 1880. A huge, old red barn loomed behind it and all sat in the middle of 20 acres of asparagus. The farm was hard work. We all worked, my parents, all of us kids, and farmworkers that came seasonally. Our dad told us, "You are no better than the workers, now get out there and work and learn Spanish while you're at it." After the season, my dad would till up the fields with "Ollie" (it was an Oliver brand tractor) and we'd walk in the powder dust picking up asparagus roots that looked like some kind of tempura mass, take them to the barn and sort them. I can still feel the dry, chalky dirt on my hands. I carried asparagus in big, brown paper grocery bags and sold it to the teachers at school. I remember scrawling Asparagas, spelled wrong, on the side of the bag with a marker and thought I was a bit of a hot shot with this product to sell to the teachers.

My dad was always fond acquiring big equipment, trucks, tractors (anything with wheels he called "rolling stock") and purchasing land with or without buildings on it. He always named the rolling stock. He brought home a semi-truck on a whim because he thought it would be fun to drive truck. My mom looked out the front window and saw a semi parked in front of the house. My dad bought an old commercial fishing boat called The Sea Fox that he brought up the Columbia to the Tri-Cities from the Pacific Ocean at the Washington and Oregon border. My mom says, "Jack never saw a utility trailer that he didn't like."

Around this time my dad was in donnybrook with a neighbor to our asparagus farm. The original farm was built by some German immigrants, the father Emil Albright. Our farm had been in the middle of 100 acres before we got it, but the outer edges had been parceled off and sold in little lots to make a trailer court. My dad's fight with the neighbor was about my brother Mike walking across the corner of his property on the way home from school or the track. When my younger brother was in grade school he'd walk up to the horse track, Sundowns Raceway, about two miles away and get grownups to place bets for him. He was lucky and won quite a bit of money. My parents had no idea that Mike was up at the track. On the way back one day, he stepped on the neighbors land. The guy threatened to actually kill Mike for stepping on his property and Mike came home scared and crying. My dad went nuts. He drove the white with turquoise stripe, old Ford pickup up on the man's lawn to his front step, then got out screaming at the neighbor's door. I'm sure our dad had a gun. The guy didn't open the door and never bugged Mike again.

My dad hated to not have control over situations that involved the safety and well-being of his loved ones. When we travelled as a family every summer throughout Canada and the west of the US growing up, he always took a handgun under the seat of the van. I thought that was a pretty badass Clint Eastwood- Dirty Harry thing to do. Dad always liked to drive because he thought he was the safest driver. My dad was not a good flier for a similar reason, he hated to relinquish control to the pilot. He really avoided airplane travel as much as possible. He always wanted to travel to the Old Country and see Ireland and Scotland where his parents and Jim were from but would not take the plunge and fly there.

So in the mid-1980s, I started getting him gifts related to the Old Country for his birthdays and Christmas. When I lived in Seattle, I got him a Scotch-plaid wool slouch hat at a downtown haberdashery that looked like Pawn's hat. Pawn was actually buried with his plaid hat in his hands. For another I got him a big coffee table book of beautiful Irish scenic photos, he'd look through it and say wistfully, "This is the closest that I will ever get to the Old Country." I got him a subscription to the Irish tourism magazine "Ireland of the Welcomes,"[40] and looking through he'd say the same thing, "This is the closest that I'll ever get to the Old Country." My elder brother and I would offer to take him and our mom to the damned Old Country and he would never agree to it. We said more than once, "Dad, let's go to Northern Ireland and see Slemish Mountain where Grandma Jean was born." He'd say every time, "Jeezus Christ, why in thee hell would I want to go up there and get caught in the goddamned crossfire?" End of discussion. He was talking about the "Troubles" in Northern Ireland, the sectarian violence that went on for 30 years, and I guess he had a point at the time.

In the late 1990s, during the Riverdance "Lord of the Dance" Irish dancing sensation in the US– he got tickets for just me and him and we went to a local performance by the traveling troupe. He was moved by the music and dancing just like me and said after, "Now THAT is the closest I'll ever get to the Old Country." Dad was very dramatic about some things and this was one of them. He always had plenty of money and time to do everything that he wanted to do. Our dad was an asparagus farmer, then a successful construction contractor (another Irish American cliché) and he was fully retired at age 55. Dad could have gone to Ireland and Scotland, sure, he did exactly what he wanted. Famous Jack quote, "I'm not gonna punch a goddamned time clock for anyone!" He hunted, fished, boated, traveled in the west and Canada, golfed, enjoyed his life and his family. But never got to the Old Country. So I kept on with the Irish and Scottish themed gifts, subscribed him to "Irish America" magazine – got him a CD of Irish folk songs for his car – many tins of Walkers shortbread and so on.

My dad and I loved the Godfather movies.[8] We watched them together many times and we could each quote lines from the iconic immigrant story. In the early 1990s, we'd do a marathon of all the Godfathers in a row. We called it "Iron-manning the Godfather." He and I both loved The Godfather I and II, the Godfather III not so much, but when it came out we added it to the marathon. Around this time, my dad bought me a musical jewelry box that plays the waltz theme from the Godfather –from the wedding scene when Connie Corleone got married.

All my life, my dad used Yardley English Lavender soap, and had a faint hint of that and chewing tobacco around him when you moved in close to talk or give him a hug. My dad was a good hugger; I still remember hugging him and his cold white cotton Hanes tee shirt under my hands on his back and cold on my cheek on his shoulder. He wasn't that tall so hugging him was easy.

In the mid-90s, when I graduated from a university, my dad was proud and acted like I was the first person to ever do so in the history of higher education. When I got married and had two kids in the latter 90s my dad thought I was a great wife and mother – I actually was. Jack was my number one fan and I was his: the mutual admiration society. I think this was a little sickening to my three brothers. But my dad "got" me; he was the one who fully understood me. My dad taught me to see humor in everything, that is his legacy in me. We'd especially break out the black humor when something was really bad or hopeless.

My father was generous to a fault and took care of people all through his life: family, friends, even acquaintances of a few minutes. He always carried around a wad of money in the 1980s and on, when he had money to spare, like $2000 cash, in case someone needed something. But he was discreet, didn't flash it around like some high roller. And he always operated with cash, not credit. My dad got burned plenty of times by acquaintances that didn't pay back – and he didn't even care or keep score, but helped many more with his emergency loans. For his kids and grandkids, he'd fold up a bill, like a $100 for me and "grease" you with it, which meant secretly palm it to you. He'd tell me, "That's for being such a good daughter" or a wife or mother. When I was in high school my dad gave me 50 bucks for each A on my report card. No wonder I turned out to be such a bookish nerd. For the little grandkids he'd pull all the change out of his pockets and grease them with it in a really funny way. My dad always said, "Your money is no good here" and paid for dinners for everyone he sat down with, for decades.

He was the common denominator in many scuffles, but helped many people too. Jack's humanitarian work included: Letting an outlaw Gypsy Joker biker that worked for his construction company live in his warehouse in a store room. Then there was Felix and his family that picked our asparagus, my dad took care of them. Felix would say, "Jake, I need you to get my son out of jail just one last time." My dad's kindness brought our Portuguese friend Wayne Sloan from California to live in our farmworker's cottage when Wayne came in the firehouse and needed a hand. Sloan (as my dad called him) became dad's best friend for life: his best "Portagee" friend. My dad paid for a friend of my brothers' to go to college because he thought the boy deserved a chance. A friend of ours, Warren Dykeman, said that Jack McCleary "was a role model to many, not just his own kids."

As an older man Jack reminded me of Robert Duvall on Lonesome Dove,[41] (the other set of movies that we loved to watch together) his speech patterns, look and demeanor, but with shockingly blue eyes - especially if he wore a blue shirt. My dad wasn't an active cowboy but would wear a nice beige felt Stetson if he took a mind too; guys do that out here in the west. Jack (he was called Cactus Jack by most, or just Cactus) had lots of folksy sayings that he flung around, some cute and some a little offensive. If someone, close friend or acquaintance, gained weight he'd say, "Christ man, you're big enough to butcher!" (we hated that one) or "it looks like you've wintered well." If a sex scene came on a TV show, his classic response was, "Jeezus Christ, enough with the goddamn gymnastics!" in a feigned semi-disgusted tone. Uncle Howard disturbingly calls sex, "Doing the dipsy-doodle." My dad didn't say "See you later" but, "See you somewhere down the trail." If you were slow bringing something: "Are you bringing that by goddamned pack mule?" Riding in the car on family vacations fighting amongst ourselves: "Christ, look out the window and learn something!" If you needed to change a plan midstream, "Make a field correction." "When the smoke clears"; there are a million of his sayings. My favorite: "This life is not a goddamned dress rehearsal."

Aunt Dona says, "Brother Jack could make a rock laugh." He saw it as a challenge and honed his craft from his teens on. Uncle Howie says if there was any asskicking to be done he would do it; if there was a story to be told he always deferred to Jack, my dad. That's how the labor was divided between the brothers. Since my dad died I love to see my grizzled old uncle; he reminds me of my dad very much. Howard has the same sarcastic, smart-ass sense of humor, the same blue eyes, same mannerisms and the same unique perspective as a child of immigrants that grew up in the western US at WWII and after. They have many of the same vocabulary words only found in the McCleary catalog. Howie is a road weary, rough around the edges, Camel smoking, lounge-pant wearing version of my dad. One of my son's friends said "Who's the old guy with the funny pants?" when Howard was shuffling around here and Liam said, "Oh, that's just Uncle Howard." When my dad found out that he was dying, he was most concerned about how to tell his little brother.

Well, I guess we are at the death portion of the program. By this time some of the main players had died in addition to Grandma Jean in 1971. Uncle Jim died in 1974 at 46 years old and James "Pawn, Scotty, Buzzard" McCleary died in 1987 of natural causes at 82. When Pawn died in West Richland he was a retired Union Carpenter with 7 living children, 43 grandchildren and 28 great grandchildren. This was 1987, there are lots more of us now. Uncle Jim's death in Portland is shrouded in mystery. He was hit on the highway by a vehicle and died shortly after at the hospital. That much I know for sure. Some say he was on a bicycle and got hit by a truck, some say he was drunk or mentally ill and stumbled across the highway and got hit, some say it was suicide and that he may have jumped from the overpass into an oncoming semi-truck. Some even say that Uncle Jim was tied in with the Irish mob and this had something to do with his early demise. Several of The Aunts were able to rush to Portland and see their eldest brother in the hospital before he passed on from his injuries. Pawn was down in California visiting Bumps when the accident occurred and he rushed to Portland but Jim was gone. It was so very hard to get Jim here and such a quick exit.

In early spring of 2009, my dad got sick suddenly. I was planning on at least 20 more good years with him as were my three brothers. It never occurred to me - ever- that my dad could die; I always thought my mother would go first (she's from the Rawlings with the bad tickers), but not my dad. He always lived bravely and fiercely in the present and was very alive, "larger than life" they said. My father really seemed indestructible to me. Seems so silly now. In Seattle, he had the best care in the country from the fancy cancer doctor from Tulane University in New Orleans, and the surgeon called Dr. Andrew Ross. My dad called him Doc Ross. Most McClearys are not religious, but we believe in luck and signs in our family and dad thought it was a good sign that his doctor was called Andrew, a McCleary family name, and had the surname Ross, same last name as my kids and their dad. My dad's pale and freckly body, that was not ever burly to start with, went through so many "procedures"- a nice word for torture, that he just started to lose weight and disappear.

Doc Ross had to put a tube with a scope and some tools down my dad's throat over and over to try to fix him and release the bile that was poisoning his body because of the cancer masses. In the hospital, my dad was more concerned for us than for himself. He wanted my mom and me to go shop and enjoy Seattle like we had in the old days, not sit beside his bed in that old high-rise hospital on what they call Pill Hill on the edge of downtown Seattle. At this time, my parents had been married for 46 years. Their marriage was a success; not easy, turbulent at times, unconventional, but a successful love story nevertheless – their love story. My dad loved my mother very much, he told me so.

After one of the last heroic efforts by Doc Ross with the scope and stents, my dad woke from the sedation and sat up in the bed. His white hair was longish and his matching beard was stubbly from all this time in hospitals and no time to go to the barber. He started to talk in a gravelly, odd, deep voice that was the result of all those intrusive tubes. All of the sudden he looked at me with his old twinkly eyes and said very loud in a deep, gravelly voice, "Luca Brasi sleeps with the fishes." That was the line from the Godfather I where Abe Vagoda, with the deep voice, opens up the newspaper with the dead fish inside and tells Sonny Corleone that Brasi is dead. Dad was joking about his hoarse voice with a line from the

Godfather. We - my mom, dad and I, had a much needed laugh at the joke and his impeccable comic timing. But there was no cure for our dad and no amount of luck or synchronicity or pleading for a miracle in the Catholic Church could stop the march of the rare and aggressive pancreatic cancer. A straight-shooter to the end, in the last week of his life my dad said to me, "If there are any family secrets that you want to know about Sis, now would be the time to ask."

My dad died early that September at home in bed in the Italian-style villa out in the orchards south of town that he built for my mother. Whatever my mom wanted he delivered, always. My dad had asked me to send Doc Ross, and his staff at Virginia Mason Hospital, a Christmas card from him that year to thank them for all their skill and efforts on his behalf. So I did, and let them know that 800 people had turned out for Jack's memorial that September. The crowd included Richland Firefighters with a ladder truck and a bagpiper from The Desert Thistle Pipe Band that played Amazing Grace and other hymns as people filed in. It seems old Red McCulley, the Batt Chief, died a week before my dad. So, twice that fall, the young bucks (Jackism) from the firehouse that had heard of Red McCulley and "Cactus" Jack McCleary, shined up the ladder truck, drove to the two memorials and flew the American flag from the extended ladder for the Richland Fire Department old timers that had "gone on down the trail."

Suzanne McCleary & James McCleary -1985

Below: Jack and Beverley, back row   - 1991
Anna, Betty, Dona, Howard McCleary, front

Jack A.
McCleary,
1992

Below:
Jack and
Suzanne
McCleary on
her wedding
day, 1997

CHAPTER 12

COUNTY ANTRIM, NORTHERN IRELAND - 2010

The moist, almost wet, clear air made my long, curly hair even curlier, like it gets on the Washington coast or in Seattle. When it gets like this I call it "frizztastic" - an auburn mass that won't behave. I was thinking that the brown, well broken-in Converse sneakers that I was wearing might not be the right footwear for this occasion. Better than Kim's though, she had on blush-pink fabric Prada sneakers. She'd always been stylish all the years that I have known her since we were 12, and now we are in our 40s. Her mom was always in the clothes business, fancy clothes.

Kim wore a black fedora on our trip, way before the fedora thing was popular anywhere - this was 2010. Good God, that fedora took on a life of its own down in Dublin. Guys in the pubs, some more drunk than others, went crazy for it and took it off her head and tried it on; like they had never seen a hat before. Maybe hers was the first black fedora to come ashore to the Island of Ireland. We'd come north from Belfast, a very different city than the jovial city of Dublin. Belfast felt tough, working class and a little dangerous. When we first arrived and were exchanging our money, I said to Kim, "Wow, this city is kind of tough and scary." She replied, "I know, did you see that baby in that stroller - he looked about 70." So today we'd ridden the North Irish Rail from Belfast up to the smaller town of Ballymena to meet my brother at the train station.

On this trip to Ireland, my first, I saw a group of people that resembled us for the first time in my life: the passengers going home to Ireland, at the gate in Atlanta. A really strange moment for me, I couldn't quit staring – that one looked like my dad, my uncle, my cousin and so on. Where we live in Washington State on the mixed up and non-ethnic west coast of the US, no-one looks like us – certainly not a crowd or whole plane load of people. Many of those people had the McCleary look: pale, freckly, blue eyes, tall men with straight noses, girls and women with curly hair, not the greatest teeth in the world.

My friend, Kim, brought me on this trip and we travelled in high style. We flew First Class the whole way. I had no idea, being a Coach Class girl, what goes on when you take a left on the plane and go behind that polyester curtain. A whole different world. I was stunned by all the wine and warm nuts and dessert carts all over the front of that plane. Too bad for the peasants riding in the cattle car in the back. In First Class, we had the seats that were paired together and reclined like big LazyBoys. On the overnight trip from Atlanta to Dublin, Kim and I were across the aisle from each other. Her seatmate was an Irish guy with a serious case of the gift of the gab. My seatmate was a nice, 35ish businessman from Georgia, a pleasant family man.

At bedtime, after donning the sleeping mask and fluffy socks found in my amenities bag, I reclined and the businessman did the same. There was a little flap between us for privacy. We politely turned away from each other. In the morning, after waking kind of slumped over toward the Georgian, noticing he was facing me and awkwardly righting myself, we said a terse good morning. I leaned over to Kim and whispered, "That's the closest I've come to having sex since I've been divorced." I was a new divorcee' at the time. We landed in Dublin and took a car to the Clarence Hotel, owned by the U2 fellows. Kim booked us there after I told her that as a longtime fan, as any self-respecting Irish American should be, I wanted to see the hotel owned by Bono and The Edge. It was the beginning of an epic trip, lovely food in great restaurants, beautiful hotels - fabulous. Kim knew and loved my dad, like a dad, for 30 years and was in Paris when he died, so she brought me on this trip in his honor.

In a pub on the Temple Bar in Dublin, an area like Bourbon St. in New Orleans - partying Ground Zero, I met an old Irish guy that asked my heritage and said, "So, the better part of ya is Irish, is it?" He went on to say that those in the North of Ireland were good supporters of hurling and rugby. He didn't comment on any other qualities of the Northerners. I think he was trying to be polite. Another guy I met was from Donegal and when he heard the name McCleary he said, "Ahhh, from the North." I've seen some wild bar scenes in my day, but nothing like what I saw in Dublin. Especially the revelers from a hurling championship packed like sardines into a pub in a state of delirium - they were so happy for their team. I thought surely that the players from the winning team were in the pub and that's why everyone was going so crazy. But no, they were just watching replays on huge TV screens and were worked into a frenzy like I had never seen. I wasn't even sure what hurling was. The Palace, with its ornate carved bar, was the quintessential Irish pub, and one of the bartenders looked very much like my brother Mike.

I worked with a guy in the US from Ballymena that knew people in Ireland named McCleary; his wife worked in a McCleary hair salon in the 1970s. Malachy McAlonan told me about the area and taught me some rudimentary pronunciations before my trip to Ireland. Broughshane is "Brow-Sheeean," gate is "gee-at," Clogh sounds nothing like the word looks. Even with a little schooling, I butchered most pronunciations while in Ireland and thought I would have some sort of genetic advantage with the accent and language – not true. Others that I learned on the fly: don't call it a bathroom, it's a "toilet": Quay (as in Wellington Quay, where we stayed) is pronounced "key," for God's sake. That was a source of embarrassment for me in a few cabs - drivers looked at me with a most puzzled expression. All the best, used as a farewell, sounds like "All da best." The word "sorrrrry" with a lilting sound in Northern Ireland is used for many occasions, from "excuse me" to "hello." Some words common in American English are almost unrecognizable in an Irish brogue.

Most obvious to me, the dreaded F word is "Foooook" and barely sounds like a cuss word, it's said in such a nicer way than the harsh sounding, vulgar pronunciation in the US. "For Foooks sake" is blurted out all over Ireland and it isn't even offensive, sounds musical. Jesus as an exclamation is "Jaaaysus." A little troubling, while standing in a coffee line in the morning, a young urban-looking man said to another "How was the crack last night?" I was shocked that someone would talk so freely about crack cocaine in public. The US it is a gangland type drug and kept on the DL (downlow), as they say. It turns out "craic" pronounced crack, means the fun, good times, the revelry in Ireland. Nothing to do with drugs at all. To make understanding even more difficult, the accent in the Republic of Ireland and the accent in the North are very different from each other. Kim said a few times in a stage whisper to me, "What are they saying? These are *your* people." We all speak English - the Americans and the Irish - but at times it really didn't seem like the same language.

I quickly learned not to say I was going to the North, to Antrim or that my family was from County Antrim unless I wanted to hear a ration of shit from people. The hostility was palpable; a cab driver that said "We used to go up there and pop us some Brits." Others said scornfully, "Why would you want to go to the North?" Leftover resentment from all the years of "The Troubles." And once we got to Belfast in the North, first thing that I noticed was the flag flying going on. On streetlamps, houses, everywhere, the British flag fluttered. In the Republic of Ireland you saw the tricolor flying everywhere. It was very obvious that we had entered a different country when we arrived in Belfast, yet on the same small island. There was a little strained exchange in a Belfast antique shop when I asked the quirky owner what something said in Gaelic on an antique postcard. He said that he was sure that he didn't know, and not in a nice way.

I hadn't heard from my brother since he sent me an email in the US that said, "See you in the Motherland," and came to Ireland ahead of us. When Kim and I came down off the N. Irish Rail train, there he was and I gave him a giant hug and Kim too. My brother leaned in and said to me in a hoarse whisper, "do you have the product?" I said, "Yes, it's in this bag on my shoulder." We all walked out of the train station to his rented compact car. I put my bag in the hatchback of the Skoda and got in.

The product was in a brass vial about ten inches long with a taped on brass cap: some of our dad's ashes. His question, some of that black humor that we grew up with. We'd come to Northern Ireland to take our dad home to Slemish Mountain. He'd died exactly one year ago to the day, September 8th. He wanted his ashes scattered to the four winds, literally. Luckily (or unluckily depending on how much you like to travel), the other three winds were in the Pacific Northwest of America. One site at the headwaters of a favorite creek, another at an old Oregon cabin, some off a high bridge on the interstate over a raging river; not sure how that will work. We'll get the younger, spry twin brothers to do that one.

So we zipped along the little back roads of County Antrim between Ballymena and Broughshane in the Skoda and tried to find our way to Slemish Mountain with a map. Arriving in Broughshane, I was shocked to see a vibrant village with flowers and nice shops and people, perky people. I'd expected the village nearest Slemish Mountain to be dilapidated with maybe a couple of Quiet Man[42] cottages and old timers staggering about. At the main busy intersection, with traffic lights even, in front of the Slemish pub, a sign said Slemish Mountain this way (with arrow) and Clogh this way (another arrow). My grandma's people were from the base of the mountain and my grandpa's people are from the village down the road,

Clogh. This sign marked the crossroads of my people, the Hunters and the McClearys.

We hung a sharp right at the Slemish Pub and headed toward the mountain, in the direction of the arrow. An old stone church with graves right up under the window was on the left as we went out of the little clean, colorful town. We were looking for a mountain, and we are from Washington State with the Cascade Range and Mount frigging Rainier, so we were looking for something large. Looking out the window going down a green-lined side road it was beautiful as you would expect Ireland to be and so tranquil. I saw the cutest abandoned stone house with a patchwork of colored metal for a roof and wanted to stop, fix it up and live there for the rest of my life. Looking, looking for the mountain we saw pastures and lovely farms. Swinging around a bend, a rock wall on my right said, "Racavan Graveyard" on an old sign set into the wall. I squealed, "Stop the car, we have relatives in there!" Grandma Jean was born at Racavan, and it's all over my notes and birth and death and immigration records. I've known that word, "Racavan" for years, and I found out it comes from the Gaelic word: Rath-cabhain, and means the Fort of the Hollow. We parked on the grassy lane and got out into the beautiful Irish air, went around the rock wall and went in through an ornate metal gate. I like how it was called a graveyard not a cemetery like in the States. They called it what it was. And what it was, was amazing.

Old graves with their crumbly cement headstones all topsy-turvy were mixed in with newer graves here and there. As you picked your way along, the ground was wet and bumpy and the ubiquitous green and the graves, some huge, some flat and austere, were all around in no particular order. No tidy rows were found in the Racavan Graveyard or as the old records call it Burying Ground. It looked like they sunk a grave wherever there was room. The big family monuments had the name emblazoned across the front with angels, cherubs, Jesus statues and other religious idols peeking out from behind pillars set in marble or stone. Sitting on top of some graves there were little rusty bird-cage things that were flower holders but looked creepy. Wandering around I found a grave for the Graham family. The Grahams are from the maternal side of my grandma's family, the McAleese side. Most closely related are Elizabeth Jane Graham, James Graham and Martha Graham. The surface of the headstone was pockmarked and hard to read, but Elizabeth Jane and James Graham were buried beneath related to me through my Grandma Jean from Racavan. In quiet reverence we wandered through the small cemetery. Then we loaded up and went to look for the mountain.

Slemish Mountain is a little plug of a mountain but easy to spot as we got near because all around were fields and fences and little roads on flat land. The mountain was the only protrusion to be seen. We parked at the bottom of the hill - hell, let's just call it what is was, and went into the little unmanned visitor center. It had information on the local flora and fauna and the history of Slemish Mountain and St. Patrick. Strange to be standing on the place I had all heard about for so many years. It wasn't a note in a journal or a scribble on the back of a photo or a dog-eared postcard from 1950 in a metal shortbread box, it was a real place. Walking outside the visitors' center and looking down and around there were farms at the base of Slemish Mountain and I wondered which farmhouse my grandma was born in.

Climbing the little trail up the mountain was mossy and slick and, as I'd predicted, the Converse sneakers were not great for traction. The well-heeled Kim was having trouble too. The trail led all the way to the top of the mountain after curving around the side, but about halfway up the hill we stopped to look for a good spot to let the ashes go. My dad loved trees and on the mostly barren hill there was a small, knarled tree that looked like a fairy's home so we stopped. In front of the tree was a rocky outcropping and we stood on it and talked about Jack. Then my brother, Jon, opened the large gold metal vial and let the ashes fly in the breeze and down toward the hand stacked stone fence. Now *that* was the closest that Jack Alexander McCleary ever got to the Old Country.

Kim handed me a bouquet of red and white roses with a green bow that we'd got in a very Catholic flower shop in Belfast. Dad's favorite color was always green. I tucked the bouquet, we'd brought on the train, into the center crook in the dark, squatty fairy tree. We looked around us and some sheep had come up close to see what we were doing. They were farm sheep, with spray painted markings on their backs, but were up wandering on the mountain. We moved around and they stayed there staring at us, not spooked. There were little tiny daisies that grew low to the grass and clumps of heather around the rock peppered side hill. We stood for a minute looking at the view. My brother Jon Andrew and I hugged for a brief moment and we started to pick our way down the slick, steep mountain path holding hands. He said, "DON'T bust your ass."

CHAPTER 13

REFERENCES

Sources Cited:

1. "United States Department of Labor, Mining Safety and Health Administration. MSHA", A Pictorial Walk Through the 20th Century, *Little Miners.* At:http://www.msha.gov/CENTURY/LITTLE/PAGE11.asp Website accessed June 29, 2012.

2. "Scottish Mining" General. 1910 Housing and "Among the Fife Miners by Kellogg Durand" London, Swan Sonnenschein & Co. Ltd. 1904 paper from 1901. Available at: http://www.scottishmining.co.uk/index.html Website accessed June 29, 2012.

3. "Scotland's History: Housing" Available at: http://www.educationscotland.gov.uk/scotlandshistory/makingindustrialurban/housing/index.asp Website accessed June 29, 2012.

4. "The History Place: Irish Potato Famine" Available at: http://www.historyplace.com/worldhistory/famine/ Website accessed June 29, 2012.

5. Coffey, Michael. edited by with text by Terry Golway. Irish in America. First Edition, Disney Enterprises, Inc, 1997.

6. Borrowman, Stuart. Behind God's Back: the Story of Blackridge. Published by Blackridge, Scotland Community Council and West Lothian, Scotland Council, 2005.

7. "20th Century Ireland – Irish History" 1900-1999. Available at: http://www.yourirish.com/history/20th-century/ Website accessed June 29, 2012.

8. *The Godfather,* Francis Ford Coppola, Alfran Productions. 1972.

9. McCullough, Colleen. The Thornbirds. HarperCollins, 1977.

10. Steves, Rick. Rick Steves' Ireland 2009. Avalon Travel, a Member of the Perseus Books Group, 1700 Fourth St, Berkeley, California, 94710, 2008.

11. "History Today," A Force Divided, Policing Ireland 1900-1960 Available at: http://www.historytoday.com/brian-griffin/force-divided-policing-ireland-1900-60 Website accessed June 29, 2012.

12. "Countries and their cultures: Northern Ireland" Available at http://www.everyculture.com/No-Sa/Northern-Ireland.html#b Website accessed June 29, 2012.

13. Wallace, Robert. and by the editors of Time Life Books. The Old West: The Miners. Time Life Books, New York, 1976.

14. "Sharon's Yorkshire Terrier Puppies" – History. Available at: http://www.sharonsyorkiepuppies.com/History.html June 29, 2012.

15. "Welsh Coal Mines Forum", *The Impractical Joke* blog and string following from March 2, 2007. Available at: http://www.welshcoalmines.co.uk/forum/read.php?10,4809 Website accessed June 29, 2012.

16. 'Scottish Archive Network", Education, Coal, Coal mining 1840-1920. Available at: www.scan.org.uk Site accessed July 9, 2012.

17. "The New York Times Archive" *The Mine Rat's Instinct – An Unerring Sign of Danger in the Collieries, Robbing Pillars in the Anthracite Mines – Swarms of Fleeing Rats Foretell the Disaster.* The New York Times, published October 1889. Available at: http://query.nytimes.com/mem/archive-free/ Website accessed June 29, 2012.

18. "Scottish Mines", Available at: http://miningartifacts.homestead.com/Scottishmines.html. Website accessed June 29, 2012.

19. "Gjenvick Archives" Social and Cultural History, Passenger list, CMV Montclare, Available at: http://www.gjenvick.com/PassengerLists/CanadianPacific-CPOS/Westbound/1927-07-29-PassengerList-Montclare.htmlJ Website accessed June 30, 2012.

20. "Gjenvick Archives"- Steamship Lines, Cunard, Passenger Lists and Historical Documents. Available at: www.gjenvick.com/SteamshipLines/CunardWhiteStar/. Website accessed site accessed July 9, 2012.

21. "Ancestry.com" Available at: http://www.ancestry.com, website accessed between 2005 and 2012, general research. Communications. Public family trees. Original records, Ireland Scotland, Canada and US.

22. "Canada's Historic Places" H.E. Guppy House, Available at: http://www.historicplaces.ca/en/rep-reg/place-lieu.aspx?id=15203 website accessed June 28, 2012.

23. "The Henry Ford Estate", Available at: http://www.henryfordestate.org/ website accessed June 28, 2012

24. "Michigan History": I think Mr. Ford is Leaving us. article by Don Lochbiler/Special to the News From the Detroit News. Available at: http://apps.detnews.com/apps/history/index.php Website accessed June 29, 2012.

25. "Historic Sites," Fair Lane where Henry and Clara Ford called home http://corporate.ford.com/our-company/heritage/historic-sites-news/historic-sites-news-detail/662-fair-lane Website accessed June 29, 2012.

26. *Butte America: the Saga of a Hard Rock Mining Town.* Pamela Roberts. 2009 (DVD) Available at: http://butteamericafilm.org/contact/purchase-home-dvd/

27. *Irish in America.* Aidan Quinn narrator. History Channel, A&E, 1995 (DVD)

28. McGrath, Jean. edited by. Butte's Heritage Cookbook. Presented by the Butte-Silver Bow Bi-Centennial Commission, Butte, Montana, 59701.

29. "Montana Historical Society," Ellen Baumler, *Devil's Perch: Prostitution from Suite to Cellar in Butte, Montana.* Available at: http://www.montanahistoricalsociety.com/education/cirguides/Baumler%20Butte%201998.pdf website accessed June 30, 2012.

30. "The Dumas Brothel Museum" Available at: http://www.butteamerica.com/dumas.htm Website accessed June 27, 2012.

31. "Ancestry.com " Montana Standard Newspaper 1938-1945, Available at: http://search.ancestry.com/browse/viewNEWS-MT-MO_ST._website accessed 2010-2012.

32. *Remembering Columbia Gardens*, Ray Ekness. Montana PBS, University of Montana. 1999.(DVD)

33. *Irish America Magazine*. Irish America Magazine, Inc. 875 Avenue of the Americas # 2100, New York, NY 10001-3586.

34. Atomic Heritage Foundation. B-Reactor: First in the World. Atomic Heritage Foundation, Richland Operations Office, prepared for the U.S. Department of Energy's Richland Operations Office. 2007.

35. Gibson, Elizabeth. Images of America, Richland Washington. Arcadia Publishing, Charleston, South Carolina, 2002.

36. "Black Past, Remembered and Reclaimed", Katie D. Morgan. Available at: http://www.blackpast.org/?q=aaw/barton-katie-d-morgan-1918-2010 Website accessed June 30, 2012.

37. Columbia River Exhibition of History Science & Technology, compiled by. ABC Homes, the Houses that Hanford Built: A to Z House Plans. 95 Lee Blvd. Richland, Washington, (509) 943-9000, www.crehst.org. No date.

38. Mahar, Margaret. "Blasted in a Radiation Accident Eight Years Ago, Harold McCluskey Is Still the Hottest Human Alive." People Magazine. December 03, 1984: Vol. 22 No. 23.

39. Watts, James. The Animal. Etcetera Press, 2009.

40. *Ireland of the Welcomes*. Irish Tourist Board: Bord Failte-Irish Tourist Board. Dublin, Ireland, 1952-.

41. *Lonesome Dove*. Larry McMurtry. Rhi Entertainment, 2008. (DVD)

42. *The Quiet Man*. John Ford. Arogosy Pictures.1952.

Bibliography:

Print sources:

Doig, Ivan. <u>Worksong</u>. Riverhead Hardcover, 2010.

Leskovar, Christy. <u>One Night in a Bad Inn: a True Story by Christy Leskovar</u>. Pictorial Histories Publishing Co. Inc. 713 S. Third Street West, Missoula Montana, 59801. Printed in Canada, 2006.

Miller, Brenda, and Suzanne Paola. <u>Tell it Slant: Creating, Refining and Publishing Creative Nonfiction.</u> Second Edition, McGraw Hill, 2012.

McCourt, Malachy, forward by. <u>Through Irish Eyes: A Visual Companion to Angela McCourt's Ireland.</u> Smithmark Publishers, 115 W. 18th St, New York, NY 10011, 1998.

Punke, Michael. <u>Fire and Brimstone: The North Butte Mining Disaster of 1917</u>. Hyperion, 77 W 66th st, 12th floor, New York, NY 10023, 2006, First Edition.

Rae, John. <u>Sister Genevieve: a Courageous Woman's Triumph in Northern Ireland.</u> Warner Book, an AOL Time Warner Company, 1271 Avenue of the Americas, New York, NY 10020, 2001.

Internet Sources:

"Abandoned Communities, Ayrshire." Available at: www.abandoned communities.co.uk.com . Website accessed July 9, 2012.

"Ancestry.com" Available at: http://www.ancestry.com. Website accessed 2003-2012.

"Ayrshire History." Available at: www.ayrshirehistory.org.uk . website accessed July 9, 2012.

"Back to Ethnic America": the Irish Potato Famine. Available at: http://www.digitalhistory.uh.edu/historyonline/irish_potato_famine.cfm Website accessed June 29, 2012.

"Belfast History: the Troubles." Available at: http://www.belfasthistory.net/troubles.html Website accessed June 29, 2012.

"The Braid, Mid-Antrim Museum." Genealogy, Clough graveyard internments. Available at: http://t hebraid.com/genealogy.aspx. Website accessed June 30, 2012.

"County Antrim Genealogy, Family History, Surnames and Local History", Ballymena, Available at: http://www.curiousfox.com/history_Ire/antrim_6.html. Website accessed June 29, 2012.

"Discovery Channel, Videos, Dirty Jobs, Coal Mucker", Available at: www.dsc.discovery.com/tv-shows/dirty-jobs/videos/coal-mucker.htm Website accessed July 9, 2012.

"Francis Firth, Nostalgic Photos, Maps, Books and Memories of Britain": Harthill. Available at: http://www.francisfrith.com/harthill,lanarkshire/#utmcsr=google.com&ut mcmd=referral&utmccn=google.com Website accessed June 30, 2012.

"Grosse Pointe Historical Society", Ford Family, Available at: www.gphistorical.org website accessed July 9, 2012.

"Ireland: society & economy", 1912-49, Available at: http://multitext.ucc.ie/d/Ireland_society__economy_1912-49 Website accessed June 30, 2012.

"Lanarkshire Mining Industry: History of Mining" Available at: http://www.sorbie.net/lanarkshire_mining_industry.htm Website accessed June 29, 2012.

"Mining Heritage Trust of Ireland", Mine Inventory: Antrim, Broughshane and Clough. Available at: www.mhti.com/mineinventory.htm#Antrim Website accessed July 9, 2012.

"Museum of the Scottish Shale Oil Industry" History. Available at: www.scottishshale.co.uk Website accessed July 9, 2012.

"NQ Higher, Scottish History", Migration and Empire, 1830-1939 The experience of immigrants in Scotland, Irish emigration to Scotland in the 19th and 20th centuries Available at: http://www.educationscotland.gov.uk/higherscottishhistory/migrationand empire/experienceofimmigrants/irish.asp "Website accessed June 29, 2012.

"People - Scots of Windsor's Past", Available at: http://www.windsorscottish.com/pl-lp-others.php Website accessed June 29, 2012.

"Scotland's Places" Available at: http://www.scotlandsplaces.gov.uk/search_item/index.php?service=RCA HMS&id=131069 Website accessed June 29, 2012.

Personal Interviews:

James "Pawn or Scotty" McCleary, 1986

Jack A. McCleary, 2006

Betty McCleary Roether, 2006

Dona McCleary Belt, 2011

Howard D. McCleary, 2011-12

Beverley McCleary Raffety, 2012

Linda Rawlings McCleary, 2012

Jim Watts, 2012

ABOUT THE AUTHOR

A second generation Irish-American, Suzanne McCleary holds a Bachelor of Arts in English with a Writing Concentration (1994) from Western Washington University in Bellingham. A lifelong resident of the Pacific Northwest, she lives on the east side of Washington State with her family. This is her first book.

Kimberly Teske Fetrow/imageworks

77643838R00088

Made in the USA
Middletown, DE
23 June 2018